Depressed?

Here is

Hugh Louis Smith ~~~~ in November 1939 in the small town of Prince ~~~~ Indiana, USA.

He studied for the Roman Catholic priesthood and was ordained a Benedictine Missionary/Monk in 1966. Most of his adult life has been spent working with Native American people, developing Native Leadership both among the Objibway in North Dakota and among the Dacotah (Sioux) in South Dakota.

He has produced various filmstrips, including *Climbing The Hill*, which treated Christian ministries and leadership from the perspective of Dacotah spirituality. He has written many journal articles, poems and short stories, as well as a novel, *Foxbarr*, which relates Native people's struggles against injustice. He has also written *Your Special Giftedness: A Spiritual Gifts Inventory*, which helps readers discover and learn how to use their special talents in Christian ministry.

He founded **Depressed Anonymous** in 1985 in Evansville, Indiana and in Louisville, Kentucky in 1986, and is the editor and publisher of *The Antidepressant Tablet* (self-help information for those depressed and for those who work and live with the depressed), located in Louisville, Kentucky. He also is in frequent contact with a number of depression self-help groups in England, Northern Ireland and South Africa.

Hugh left the active ministry in 1982 and is now a full-time counsellor with a Master's degree in Counselling Psychology earned from the University of Evansville, Indiana in 1985. He is stepfather with wife Diane and three children.

Other books by Hugh Smith

Foxbarr

Your Special Giftedness:
A Spiritual Gifts Inventory

Depressed?

Here is a way out!

by Hugh Smith, MS

edited and with a Foreword

by Dr Dorothy Rowe

FOUNT

An Imprint of **HarperCollins** *Publishing*

First published in the United States of America in 1990
by Earth and Sky Enterprises, Wilmot, South Dakota
This edition published in Great Britain in 1991 by Fount
Paperbacks

Fount Paperbacks is an imprint of Collins Religious
Division, part of the
HarperCollins Publishing Group, 77–85 Fulham Palace
Road, London W6 8JB

Phototypeset by Input Typesetting Ltd, London

Printed and bound in Great Britain by
Cox & Wyman Ltd, Reading

To my Father, Max D. Smith,
and Mother, Lorraine Louis Smith

Depressed Anonymous

MANUAL

using the suggested

Twelve-Step Programme

Contents

10   DEPRESSED?

Acknowledgements

To the many people who were once depressed and who are now leading DA groups and helping others leave the prison of depression.

For my wife Diane and her cheerful presence while I was writing this book, and to Natalie, Luke and Joseph, the children, for all their enthusiasm and support along the way.

I am extremely grateful to the many people who have made this book possible. First of all to my parents, Lorraine Louis and Max D. Smith, who have supported this work with the depressed from the very beginning. For my brother David M. Smith and his wife Susan, who made it possible for me to tell others about the hope that is there for those who work and live the 12-step programme of Depressed Anonymous.

For my long-time friend and publisher Chuck Floro, from Wilmot, SD, who has been most supportive in the various publishing projects that we have been mutually involved with.

For the original members of that first experimental DA group in Evansville, IN, who made it possible, in the Fall of 1984, to be the beginning of a DA in Evansville and Louisville, KY.

Also, I would like to thank Martha Maloney, ACSW,

my colleague at the Resurrection Counseling Center, Louisville, Kentucky, for the professional and personal positive influence that she has had on my life these past five years.

I also want to thank my friend Dorothy Rowe for her continued friendship and now for lending her expertise in the editing of this book. She is surely "carrying the message" to all those who still hurt from the painful experience of depression.

Foreword

Depression is the greatest misery, for in it we are alone in a prison from which there seems to be no escape. When we have a physical illness, no matter how great our pain, at times we can separate ourselves from our suffering and feel close to other people, sharing a joke, feeling loved and comforted. But when we are in the prison of depression we cannot separate ourselves from the depression, and there is always a barrier between ourselves and other people.

People who are depressed describe this prison in many different pictures: "I'm at the bottom of a black pit." "I'm locked in a dungeon and they've thrown away the key." "I'm inside a black balloon and as much as I struggle I can't escape." "I'm alone in an icy desert." "I'm stumbling through a black fog." "I'm wrapped in a black shroud." "I'm totally alone, and a great black bird is on my shoulders weighing me down." The pictures are many and various, but the meaning is always the same. The person is alone in a prison.

Even worse, inside the prison of depression we turn against ourselves in self-hatred. We torture ourselves with guilt and shame, fear and anger. We tell ourselves that we shall never escape from the prison, and, indeed, in some way we do not want to leave the prison. It is torture. It is safety.

The prison of depression is torture because it is isolation, the one form of torture which, as all torturers know, will break even the strongest person. But it is safety because the walls of the prison shut out most of the things which threaten to overwhelm us and cause our very self to shatter and disappear.

Many depressed people will say, "I don't know why I am depressed. It just happened suddenly, like a black cloud coming down." They say this because they do not want to look at the terrible events which threatened to destroy the way they saw themselves and their world. These events might not seem very significant to other people, but to the person concerned they are very important. It is not the events in themselves which make them important, or frightening, or overwhelming, but the meaning we give to these events.

We live in the world of meaning which we have created. Indeed, as individuals, we *are* our world of meaning. This is why, when we discover a serious discrepancy between what we thought reality was and what it actually is, we feel that our very self is being overwhelmed, is shattering, disappearing.

With this sense that our self is being annihilated comes the greatest fear, the worst fear we can know. It is greater than the fear of death, for we can face death courageously when we feel that some important part of us – our soul or spirit, or our children, or work, or just the certainty that people will remember us – will continue on. But when we feel that it will be as if we never existed, then we feel the utmost terror.

We have to defend ourselves against this terror. In my book *Beyond Fear* I have described the many defences we can use. One of the most popular defences is depression. Indeed, the human race would not have survived if we did not have the capacity to get depressed. In the safety of the prison of depression we give ourselves the time and space where we can review the situation, and see whether we can arrive at a meaning for ourselves and our life which will allow us to go on with our lives and to live in some degree of safety and happiness.

This is why many people regard their experience of depression as the most important time in their life, for out of that experience they gained great wisdom.

However, many people are not able to do this because to review their life they have to remember many painful events and question the actions of those people who should have cared for them. Too frightened to question, they willingly accept the advice of their doctors (who are also frightened to question their own lives) that they have a physical illness, and that the best treatment is pills and electroconvulsive therapy (ECT).

Fortunately, an increasing number of depressed people are realizing that, while making a journey of self-discovery on your own is difficult, making such a journey in the company of other people is a rich, fulfilling experience, and leads to enlightenment. These other people might be therapists and counsellors, or they may be people who have made, or are making, their own way out of the prison of depression.

What we need to look at and question in our lives is how we learned to think of ourselves as being unacceptable, perhaps even bad, and needing to work hard to be good. We certainly did not think that about ourselves when we were born.

At workshops on depression I ask the people there to remember an incident in childhood which led them to draw the conclusion that they were bad and unacceptable. Only those people who wish to insist that they had a *perfectly* happy childhood and that their parents were *absolutely perfect* cannot do this. Such people are few. Most people recall incidents which now might seem funny but then, and now, are sad. All children suffer so much pain and humiliation, even at the hands of parents who love them and want only the best for them.

The way children cope with pain and humiliation and the feeling that they are bad and unacceptable is to promise themselves that, if they work hard at being good, when they grow up they will be rewarded. Indeed, this is what their parents and teachers tell them. They say, "If you are bad you will be punished and if you are good you will be rewarded." Some parents say this in the context of, "This is how this family operates," but most parents and all religions expect children to learn this, not just as a rule to follow at home and at school, but as the principle on which the universe is built. We are taught that the universe is constructed on a Grand Design where goodness is rewarded and badness punished. Just what the rewards and punishments will be varies from one religion to another (a good Muslim goes to Paradise, a good Hindu is reborn as a wealthy man, a bad Christian goes to hell, a bad Jew incurs Jehovah's wrath), but the message of all religions is the same. If you are good, you will be safe and rewarded. If you are bad, bad things will happen to you.

Such children who absorb this teaching (and most do) become obedient and good. This means that they have to give up much of what they want to do and be, but they comfort themselves that by being good they will be safe and that their rewards will come.

All of this children work out in the context of planning what their life will be. We all do this in childhood, some of us very specifically, some of us in very general terms. We create a life project which is a mixture of what we would like to do and be, what our family wants us to do and be, what options we have, and how we see we can get our just rewards. Most girls create a life project built on the promise, "If you are feminine, unassertive, unselfish and attractive one day Mr Right will come along, fall in love with you and marry you, and then you'll live happily ever after." Most boys create a project built on the promise, "If you are strong, masculine and competitive you will win the prizes of women, wealth, and power, and other men will admire you."

So, having created our project we set out to live it.

If we are very, very, very lucky the life we live coincides with the project we have created. Very few of us are so lucky. Most of us discover, sooner or later, that there is a discrepancy between what we thought our life would be and what it actually is.

For some of us the discrepancy is not so great, and we can find ways of living with it. Some women discover that their marriage is not happiness ever after, but they console themselves by accepting that their husband, though boring, is a good man and worth putting up with for the sake of the children. Some men discover that not winning all the glittering prizes does not matter if you have mates, a sport to follow, and a comfortable home.

But for many of us the discrepancy is too big, too serious to be smoothed over by consolations, because the cause of the discrepancy is a disaster.

Sometimes the disaster creeps up on us slowly, as gradually the evidence mounts that our expectations of rewards are not going to be fulfilled. Perhaps we gradually discover that our marriage is cruel and destructive, or that the job we worked so hard to get is stultifying and meaningless, or that no matter how good we are our parents will never tell us that they love us unconditionally. Sometimes the disaster comes suddenly with a death, or loss, or when we are betrayed, rejected, abandoned by those most dear to us.

When disaster strikes us we cry, "I've been good all my life. Why did this happen to me?"

If we believe in the Grand Design of the universe, where goodness is rewarded and badness punished, there are only two answers we can give. Either the Grand Design was not operating properly, other people are to blame, and we have been treated unjustly. Or the Grand Design was operating properly and we are wicked and deserve our punishment.

If we choose the first answer we feel anger, resentment and bitterness. If we choose the second we feel guilt and shame.

Alternating between these answers, we find all these terrible feelings crowding in on us.

Someone may suggest to us a third answer, that the disaster happened by chance. If this is so, does this mean that no amount of goodness prevents disaster? How can I protect myself in a world where disasters can happen by chance? If things can happen by chance, is there no Grand Design? Did my parents and teachers lie to me?

To put an end to this terrifying confusion and the feeling that our very self is shattering and disappearing, we can opt for one answer, "It was my fault and I deserve my punishment," and so, turning on ourselves, cut ourselves off from everybody and everything, and find a barren safety in the prison of depression.

To find our way out of the prison of depression we

have to recover the sense of acceptability and worth with which we were born. We cannot do this so long as we cling to the belief in the Grand Design of rewards and punishments, for as much as we tell ourselves we are acceptable and valuable we shall continue to take *personally* all the cruelty and injustices we have suffered, and so long as we take these personally we shall be trapped by anger, bitterness and resentment, just as seeing ourselves as deserving punishment traps us in guilt and shame. To give up taking the cruelty and injustices we have suffered personally, we have to see ourselves, not as a tragic victim of a malign fate, but as simply unlucky. We were unlucky to have been born into that particular family at that particular time (the family would, however, have treated any baby born to them then in the same way as we were treated), unlucky to have met certain people, been in certain places. Nevertheless, having been unlucky in the past does not mean that we shall always be unlucky. In a universe where things happen by chance we can always be lucky.

To give up our belief in the Grand Design of rewards and punishments we have to make the journey which many religious people, down the centuries, have made. We have to move from the security of the fundamentalist interpretation of the religion to the freedom of the mystical interpretation of the religion.

Every religion has its fundamentalists and its mystics. The fundamentalists interpret their religion in terms of a set of absolute laws which punish the bad and reward the good and which represent the known will of the Supreme Power, God or Allah. The mystics do not have a set of absolute laws (this is why the fundamentalists disapprove of the mystics and often persecute them), and they see the Supreme Power as something or someone who is essentially unknowable but who should be taken on trust. This Supreme Power is not engaged in watching us and keeping a tally of our good and bad deeds but is simply all around us and within us. All we have to do is to let ourselves become aware of this Divine Presence, something we can do with prayerful meditation, and then, as Julian of Norwich said, "All shall be well, and all shall be well, and all manner of things shall be well."

Many people who are not at all religious have arrived at this same understanding. They experience themselves as being part of everything that is and, while they know that they can never know all that is, they live within the great Oneness with trust and acceptance.

People arrive at this acceptance, trust and understanding in many different ways. Some arrive there through suffering and trying to understand their suffering. Hugh Smith is one such person. Some arrive through the kind of spiritual awareness which Alister Hardy and David Hay have described in their research into religious or spiritual experiences which "gave a deep awareness of a benevolent non-physical power which appears to be partly or wholly beyond and far greater than the individual self". Some arrive there through sudden insight. One of my friends unlocked the door of her prison of depression when she realized that being loved by God, which she had never doubted all through her suffering, was identical with loving yourself.

In his book *The Perennial Philosophy* Aldous Huxley showed how this knowledge of oneness, belonging, no strife or striving, has been described in many different ways, using different kinds of language. We each need to find our own language, and to acknowledge that what we know can be expressed in many different ways. Hugh

Smith uses the language of Christianity, while I find the words of the *Tao te Ching* come closest to what I feel.

> Express yourself completely,
> then keep quiet.
> Be like the forces of nature:
> when it blows, there is only wind;
> when it rains, there is only rain;
> when the clouds pass, the sun shines through.

> If you open yourself to Tao,
> you are at one with the Tao
> and you can embody it completely.
> If you open yourself to insight
> you are at one with insight
> and you can use it completely.
> If you open yourself to loss,
> you are at one with loss
> and you can accept it completely.

> Open yourself to the Tao,
> then trust your natural responses;
> and everything will fall into place.

Once we have reached such an understanding and acceptance we want to help other people to find this too. I do this chiefly through writing, but Hugh Smith does so by action, by engaging people in dialogue, and by getting depressed people to do what they least want to do: to come out of their isolation, to share their experiences with others, and to become concerned with and involved in the lives of other people.

When I first began researching in depression, back in 1968, the only treatment depressed people got from psychiatrists was pills, ECT and psychosurgery, where incisions were made in the frontal lobes of their brain. My research required that I should talk to depressed patients, and, lo and behold, many of these patients got better. This was not because I had some magic cure, but because, for the first time, these people were able to tell their story to someone who was concerned and interested. By telling their story they found that their lives gained in significance, and by explaining the whys and hows to someone who was not always sure that she understood, they worked out better choices for themselves, and went on with their lives.

In 1972 I went to Lincolnshire, and there I met a most remarkable young woman, Jackie Childs, who, having been depressed and experienced the horrors of an old-fashioned psychiatric hospital, decided that she would try to help depressed people to avoid such suffering by starting a self-help group. I badgered several of my clients into joining, and I followed the progress of the group over several years. I saw many people who spent some time in this group change enormously and take charge of their lives.

At the same time two organizations, **Depressives Associated** and **Depressives Anonymous**, were established in the UK. Depressives Associated, led by the courageous Janet Stevenson who, alas, died in 1990, became a network of people who kept in touch by meetings, letters and telephone, and now a newsletter. Depressives Anonymous developed a technique for self-help therapy, and has been a resounding success.

I first met Hugh Smith when I was in the USA for a lecture tour in 1986. He invited me to meet the Depressed Anonymous group he had set up in Evansville, Indiana, and we have kept in touch ever since.

There is no need for me to describe what a warm, loving, passionate person Hugh is, because that shines through every page of this book. Nor need I say what a pleasure it is to write a foreword to it, because simply knowing that this book is now available to a wide range of readers instead of to the lucky few who can join a Depressed Anonymous group and work with Hugh is a great pleasure in itself.

Self-help groups for the miseries which plague us can be organized and run successfully in many different ways. Hugh, knowing the success of the methods used by Alcoholics Anonymous, adapted these to the problems faced by people who are depressed, particularly those who have been depressed for a long time.

This book offers a framework for setting up and running such a self-help group which can be adapted to the special needs and circumstances of many different people. It can be used as a blueprint for a group or as a study book for an individual. It offers a set of steps and an inexhaustible source of ideas for meditation and discussion. It shows how we can all experience "the miracle of the group". Most of all, it shows how we can discover the essential unity of loving and accepting ourselves and one another, of being close to others, and experiencing the sense of oneness in all in which we can reside in acceptance and trust.

Once we know this, we know that we cannot avoid disaster simply by being good. Since we live on a planet which is not particularly hospitable to us, since we cannot separate ourselves from nor control the political and economic forces of our world, since not all our plans will come to fruition, since events beyond our control may take our loved ones away from us, and old age and death, like taxes, are inevitable, we cannot avoid disaster. But now we are free of the burden of trying to ward off disaster by being good, and we can be good simply because it pleases us to do so. Now we are free of the burden of feeling that we have to pay for every bit of good fortune which befalls us with acts of goodness and a feeling of unworthiness, and we can simply enjoy our good luck. And when disaster strikes, we do not have to ask ourselves what wickedness we have committed. Instead, we meet disaster with courage and with the love and support of our friends.

Dorothy Rowe

Gloria's Story

Dear Hugh,

I'm going to make an attempt to write what DA has done and continues to do for me and, through me, my family. Forgive my bad grammar – it's from the heart!

I remember my first night at a *Depressed Anonymous* meeting. It was 6th June 1985. I went into the room of people I didn't know, afraid. I wondered what it would be like and sat at the back so I could leave if I wanted to! I was withdrawn with the pain of depression so I knew I wouldn't open my mouth to these people I didn't know. The man in charge took me out to another room and asked me a few questions. I found out later it was to see if I needed medical care. When it came my turn to talk at the group of nine people, I refused. Everyone had a story, very sad, to tell. When I came home I decided I didn't need to hear any more sadness so I wouldn't return the next Thursday night, and I didn't. But, by the next Thursday I was ready to go try again.

After my fourth Thursday, I opened up a little. I didn't trust these people yet. As the Thursdays passed, I became more relaxed and realized they could become good friends to me. I felt a closeness to these people and I've always liked helping others, so I opened up more and more and more.

After meetings we would go to a restaurant for coffee and food. One night I was laughing and talking, and our Counsellor in Charge said, "Gloria, you have opened up like a rose. Petal by petal you have opened up." Well, I felt special and very good inside. It had been a lot of work and it was noticed by him. I felt proud.

I've gone through a lot of heartache this last five years. Eye surgery, mother's death, my grandson's wreck, husband's death, and I'm in the process of bringing my grandson back from the hell of drugs, alcohol and Satanism.

I moved to Evansville ten years ago. It is hard to make friends in a new city. But through my support groups and church, I have made lots of friends, super-friendly people.

DA is now meeting at a church on Washington Avenue. I'm a facilitator when I am needed. Something I never thought I could do five years ago!! I pray before I go to meetings and ask God to speak through me to help these people. I always go to a new person, as I vividly remember my first meeting, and make them feel welcome.

There are four of us who were there together first on 6th June 1985. We have become very good friends. I still remember the things the Counsellor from the very first meeting told us. I've seen people come and go, some helped, some for just one meeting, some wanting a magic wand waved! To me, it has helped me over the rough spots, giving me courage to go on as a widow. I have found a peace in life. A special joy in knowing and loving people. In helping others I have helped myself.

I know my background in life has made me depressed at times. My mother was abusive and I realized later in life it was an emotional illness. I forgave her.

I will continue to attend DA. Every meeting is different and who knows what mystery each group holds! Who needs me, who needs a smile or hug, who needs to feel they are not alone, who needs to know there is a God who loves us all.

My love and prayers,
Gloria

Introduction

Depression

and the Higher Power

Katie was brought to her first *Depressed Anonymous* meeting by her son. She had attempted suicide twice and just had given up on life. She was sick and tired of being sick and tired. She felt alone and worthless. The son knew that this was a last chance for his Mum and so he literally forced her to the meeting. Katie was very nervous and as she looked around at the group she wondered how she could get up and leave without too much attention being drawn to her leaving. She stayed on, and the more she listened the more she found that the members of this group were speaking her language – the language of the pain and isolation of depression. She stayed and kept coming back to meetings. Within a year she was leading her own group in another part of town.

Don said that he had been depressed from the time he was born. He always felt empty inside and never felt anyone really understood what he was feeling. He felt angry but believed it was sinful to express it. He stuffed it inside himself instead. He came to a few meetings and gradually felt that someone was hearing him. No one advised him to "snap out of" his depression, like so many other family members and friends had. Don gradually started to feel better the more he came to the group, admitted his life was unmanageable and then turned his life over to the care of God, the Higher Power *as he understood Him to be.*

Joe felt that the *Depressed Anonymous* group were a bunch of sad sacks who met and talked to each other about how sad they felt. He didn't want anything to do with those long faces and sad tales – his life was bad enough without having to listen to everyone else's problems. That was the way he felt before attending a meeting. To test out his hypothesis he went to one meeting. He believed it to be such a positive experience that he has continued and now serves as leader of the group! In DA Joe feels everyone is speaking the same language of pain, isolation and the fatigue that most people who are depressed experience at one time or another.

As a counsellor I see it as my job to help people like Katie, Joe and Don help themselves to recovery. Often my clients are referred to other twelve-step self-help groups of people dependent upon their particular compulsion/addictions. Most people have been hurt in the midst of their family of origin and so the twelve-step group represents a potential new "surrogate" family where the hurting member can learn new behaviours, be accepted for who he/she is, while possibly for the first time in his or her life be nurtured back to life and healing. Nothing could be more supportive than to provide a group of men and women with a means to encourage their commitment to growth.

The twelve steps are the essential beliefs of **Alcoholics Anonymous**, a recovery programme originally developed to help men and women deal with their addiction to alcohol, one day at a time. The twelve steps have been found to be a potent means of recovery for those who desire to free themselves from their compulsions. The twelve steps are basically a programme of letting go of our compulsions and handing over our will to the care of God.

Many people get organized religion and spirituality mixed up and DA achieves strength from spirituality without set creed, dogma or doctrine. All the programme asks is that the person who comes to the meeting has a sincere desire to stop the compulsion. In the case of *Depressed Anonymous*, a person must have a sincere desire to stop "sadding" oneself, that is, making oneself feel sad.

Members of twelve-step groups make no apologies for faith in a God that can restore one not only to sanity but to serenity and joy as well. "We never apologize for God. Instead, we let Him demonstrate, through us, what He can do. We ask Him to remove our fear and direct our attention to what He would have us be. At once, we commence to outgrow fear." (1)*

We read many times that fear and anger are the greatest causes of depression, and the twelve-step programme attacks both these unpleasant emotions head on.

Dorothy Rowe, in her award-winning book *Depression: The Way Out Of Your Prison* (17), describes how people build their prisons of depression by holding the following six beliefs as though they were real, absolute and immutable truths.

1 No matter how good and nice I appear to be, I am really bad, evil, valueless, unacceptable to myself and to others.

2 Other people are such that I must fear, hate and envy them.

* Figures in brackets refer to the bibliography at the back of the book.

3 Life is terrible and death is worse.

4 Only bad things happened to me in the past and only bad things will happen to me in the future.

5 Anger is evil.

6 I must never forgive anyone, least of all myself.

These are the six main ingredients of depression. These beliefs, tenaciously held, imprison the depressed until that day when they make a decision to choose to remove the bars.

Dorothy Rowe, a clinical psychologist from England, has written eight books which deal with depression, and is an international figure who is deeply concerned with the worldwide prevalence of depression. She also believes that depression is not a disease or an illness but is a human experience that is truly painful and isolating in nature. She points out that the belief that depression is a physical illness has the good implication that we are not to blame for our depression but the *bad implication* is that we could get it again, like a bout with the flu or another cold. Psychiatrists who believe that depression is a physical illness don't talk about curing depression but about *managing* it.

The *bad implication* for depression, using a psychological model, is that we caused it ourselves – by the way we think (our six immutable truths), live out our lives, and reflect on our world. But the *good implication* of this psychological model is that if we caused the depression we can likewise undepress ourselves. This is the approach Dorothy Rowe takes. This is why she calls depression a moral problem – we have to take full responsibility for the way we think, feel and act.

Depressed Anonymous bases its healing and recovery on

the premise that once depressed persons admit that they are out of control, even to the extent of attempting suicide, they then come to believe that a power greater than themselves can restore them to sanity, while at the same time making a decision to turn their minds and wills over to the care of God as they understand Him.

The God as we understand Him is what appeals to more and more persons as they admit their helplessness over their compulsive/depressive thoughts, actions or behaviour which they feel they no longer have any power to control.

The twelve-step programme helps people to become God-conscious. It is in working the programme, while making no excuses for the spiritual nature of our recovery, that we can attribute our new-found sense of hope and peace to the Higher Power. For the active member of *Depressed Anonymous* there begins to glimmer in the distance the bright light of hope.

By recognizing how it feels to be depressed more people will have the help and guidance that will get them through their depression; lives will be saved as well.

Being depressed means *isolation*, being cut off from everybody and everything. People describe their experience of depression as being in some kind of a prison. One man said that he was in a pit where the walls were of soft clay. The more he tried to climb up, the more he slid back down. One woman said that she was in a brick maze where there was no exit and the walls were closing in on her. "I'm in an infinite desert," said one man, "there's just me and a lone, scrawny tree." "I'm in a cage," said one woman, "the bars are thick and black and there's no door." Inside this prison the person has intense feelings of self-hatred.

Inside the prison of depression the person can experience the following –

* Change of appetite.
* Changes in sleeping patterns.
* Fatigability or lack of energy; tired most of the time.
* Loss of interest in daily activities and/or decreased sex drive.
* Inability to concentrate.
* Feelings of sadness, hopelessness, worthlessness, guilt or self-reproach.
* Thoughts of suicide.
* Withdrawing from others.
* Problems with memory.
* Feeling you're losing your mind.

Frequently, depressed persons imagine they are going crazy, *are* crazy or are being afflicted with some mental illness. All of the above are not true. One of the beautiful things about a DA group is that everyone has the same symptoms, feels the same pain and is relieved that they are not the only ones in the world with this experience. They don't have to go it alone. They also don't hear people saying, "Snap out of it".

The important thing is not so much whether depression is or is not an illness or a mental disorder but that people have to take responsibility for themselves and their feelings. So many people think that since they are patients of a doctor they must sit back and wait for the medicine to kick in, without ever examining the way they think, feel or live out their lives. So often those depressed are living out of step with their own expectations or the expectations of others. It would be great if the many people on anti-depressant medication would start talking out why they depressed themselves in the first place. The pain might disappear with the medication but the experience is still part of their life.

Depressed Anonymous, once established in your community, will gradually gain new members as the word gets out that a group exists in which people who are depressed can come and share their story with others.

Besides reading the twelve steps at each meeting the group learns on a firsthand basis about "the miracle of the group". It is in the sharing of the members of the group that one's recovery begins.

It is in the group that the depressed person begins trusting other members when they say they have admitted that their lives are unmanageable, and that they have made a conscious decision to turn their lives over to God or the Higher Power. This new belief gradually removes the fear that they will never get better. So many people who are depressed believe that once they start feeling a little better it won't last, and that they will slip back into their depression. They might slip back into their old ways of thinking and acting but you don't slip back into sadness *unless you choose to do so*. We are not wanting to use language that creates an attitude in our mind that we can't make a difference in the way we feel and act. Remember, language creates our reality.

The main effect of *Depressed Anonymous* is that people can come together and find the support of fellow depressed people, and they in turn will find the emotional nurturing and acceptance, and learn the social skills that can help them gradually enter life again with hope and heightened spirit. Once people realize that they are not alone they then take hope that maybe they too will feel better. The beauty of a self-help group is that a person feels acceptance from the group. No one is there telling you to "snap out of it" or that your depression is all in your mind.

I believe that the general public needs to see that they, even though not professional therapists themselves, can still organize twelve-step self-help groups for persons in their area. Most communities are in contact with mental health specialists who would be happy to help set up self-help or support groups for community members and to meet on a weekly basis.

Depression is a growing global mental health issue, according to the World Health Organization. The Royal College of Psychiatrists estimates that one woman in four and one man in seven will experience a serious period of depression by the age of sixty-five. All of us in our communities, even though we may not be mental health professionals, can still be advocates and conveners for those people who are struggling alone with the isolating pain of depression and who would be willing to help themselves and others by forming a self-help group such as *Depressed Anonymous*.

The book you are about to read is really a statement about healing and recovery. It deals with all addictions, be it substance addiction, i.e., hooked on drugs, or a process addiction in which a person is hooked on a particular behaviour. When we talk about one addiction, like the process addiction of depression, we can include them all. What we all are learning is that the twelve-step programme of recovery can be used to overcome any compulsive/addictive behaviour for that person who sincerely wants to get emotionally, physically and spiritually healthy.

Step One

We admitted that we were Powerless over Depression – that our Lives had become Unmanageable

How often have I had people tell me that they've "suffered" from depression for as long as they could remember. They tell of the many agonizing hours, days, months and years in which they consider their depression experience as an everlasting problem. Some say that their depression is a comfort, namely, that they would be lost without that old and predictable miserable feeling they wake up to every morning. In other words, they have bought into one of the six principles of defeat experienced and lived out by persons depressing, viz., "that since bad things have happened to me in the past, bad things will happen to me in the future." They believe that what is will always be.

It is in the admission that we are out of control that a remedy can be applied to our battle with depression. It is a paradox for our understanding of depression to learn that only when we give up control do we gain control over what we want to be, think and do. If there is anything that creates a sense of hopelessness it's when we feel we don't have any control over our lives. When we are depressed we feel dependent on all the forces that act on us and our environment. We feel we are the victims of the interminable feeling that we call depression. Depression can be like a hell or a bottomless pit from which we feel we can never escape. It's like being in an eighty-foot hole with an eight-foot ladder.

Some of the major ways people help build the walls of their depression are to consider themselves worthless, they won't allow themselves to get angry, they can't forgive themselves or others, and they believe that life is bad and death is worse. Also, they believe that since bad things happened to them in the past bad things are bound to happen to them again in the future.

This is the type of thinking that we must surrender if we want to feel better. We can start enjoying a life that is meant to be enjoyed – not just endured. We especially want folks like yourself to get involved in a group that we call *Depressed Anonymous*. It is one of the better ways to realize that we can *choose* to escape the terrible personal isolation and anguish of depression. Who better knows the pain and the isolation of depression than the person who has been depressed? It is my personal conviction, both as a psychotherapist and as a person who has experienced depression, that it was only when I admitted that I was depressed that I could start working my way out of this terrible and immobilizing experience. In my own experience I thought I was losing my mind, as I couldn't cram another thought into my head and couldn't remember a thing that I had just read or thought a minute before.

I was tired all the time and would wake up early in the morning and couldn't get back to sleep. But that's the best news most people hear when they come to a *Depressed Anonymous* meeting for the first time, namely, that they are not losing their minds. When you're depressed you feel your mind is made out of cottonwool and all of life seems grey, cold and lifeless.

The important thing to remember about depression is that you are not a victim. You have bought into the belief that you can't change how you feel. You need to believe that once you change the way you think then that in itself can begin to produce a change in the way you feel.

Thoughts produce feelings which produce our behaviour. Give up the belief that you are like the helpless sailor alone in his boat on the ocean without a paddle. You are not a sailor without a paddle – you do have a paddle, but you feel that since there is no land in sight it won't make any difference for you to row anyway. So many times people who depress themselves feel that no matter what they do they will never feel better. With the twelve-step programme you can recover – although most likely not right away. Let's be honest – nothing that has taken the greater part of a lifetime to build can be dismantled in a few days or weeks. But you will feel better if you follow the instructions in this book and begin to work and live the twelve-step programme.

Persons who come to the *Depressed Anonymous* meetings soon learn that if they want to make progress and start to feel good about themselves then they have to admit that they are powerless over their depression and that their lives have become unmanageable. I might have had the thought – possibly even as I read this – that I want to end my life. Please finish reading this book before you do anything else. Others have been helped and now so can you be. You can make that decision and choose to begin to feel better. You can get out of your depression if you want to – like most depressive experiences, many are due to the way we have learned to think and act. There is no proof – again, let me repeat – there is **no** scientific proof that shows that a specific and significant change in the brain chemistry precedes and is the cause for depression. Dorothy Rowe points out that any emotion, pleasant or unpleasant, felt long enough, can produce significant physiological changes in the human body. The implication here is that if you think enough unpleasant thoughts long enough then these thoughts are bound to have some form of repercussion in the body. We are not talking here about some prescribed medications that have been known to cause the patient to feel depressed.

As mentioned earlier (p. 31) Dorothy Rowe points out that if you work out of the disease model for your under-standing of depression then the good implication is that you are not responsible for being depressed. The bad implication is that you might catch it again, like the flu or a winter cold. But Dorothy Rowe sees another model, namely the psychological model which helps us better understand the source of human depression. She says that if you operate out of the psychological model instead of the disease model then the bad implication is that you caused the depression yourself; but the good implication is that if you caused it yourself then you can *undepress* yourself. This is our position in *Depressed Anonymous*.

Depressed Anonymous is based on the twelve steps of **AA**. We grant that we are not alcoholics but we also know that our compulsive depressing thoughts and actions con-tinually reinforce our sense of worthlessness and hope-lessness.

Whenever we feel like withdrawing from an unpleasant

situation or thought we immediately medicate ourselves with an immobilizing feeling of sadness. By "medicate" I mean that we use sadness like an anaesthetic drug in that it prevents us from feeling anything other than the sadness that is ever present. Any situation that might cause us to live and think differently is sometimes cause enough for us to medicate ourselves with sadness. Many times just a thought about a past sin or fault of ours will throw us down into a spiral of self-hate and despair. We sad ourselves. Even though the twelve steps of Alcoholics Anonymous deal with a person's compulsion to drink, and those in AA unequivocally promote the idea that alcoholism is an illness, no one should feel guilty or ashamed of their addiction to alcohol because it is a disease. We in *Depressed Anonymous* do not espouse the idea that persons depressed are mentally ill. This stigma has been placed on persons depressed long enough, and it has stopped many from getting help because of the shame associated with this painful feeling.

In *Depressed Anonymous* we meet many people who come to our group expecting to hear us say that their depression is an illness or that they are sick. They will not hear that at a DA meeting. We do know that an unpleasant emotion experienced over time, such as fear, can produce metabolic changes in the human body. *Depressed Anonymous* has at its core the twelve steps and we advocate their use as the surest way out of depression. The twelve steps originated to deal with the baffling and cunning problem of alcoholism. We also see their power work for people who don't have a disease but want to get in touch with a power greater than themselves so as to recover from their crippling depression. When we tell them that just as they caused their depression they like-wise can undepress themselves we caution them that this is not intended to put them down but to give them hope. We believe that in time, and by working the programme, they will begin to feel better.

Many newcomers only know that their sadness has been a part of their life for as long as they can remember. We do not blame them for their depression. We in DA are not in the blame game – we only want to look our depression squarely in the eye and learn how to get unde-pressed. Our recovery from depression depends on our desire to quit sadding ourselves, coupled with the admission that our lives are unmanageable and that only a Power greater than ourselves can free us from our life-long prison of depression.

But don't get me wrong – I don't believe you can *snap* out of your depression, or suddenly and dramatically get your life turned around by going to one DA meeting, or reading the twelve steps five times an hour. It just doesn't happen that way, especially if you have lived with your depression for any length of time. Even though we emph-asize that your depression is not a disease we do want you to know that a depression over a long time can cause physical problems and upset the metabolism of the human organism. More and more doctors are seeing how positive feelings, attitudes and emotions can help cancer patients maintain a remission and stay free of a recurring cancer condition. Unpleasant emotions such as fear, anger, resentment, tension and depression work against recovery.

I would call this sadness that has been with us for as long as we can remember a learned way to respond to certain negative stimuli. What you will be doing when you come to *Depressed Anonymous* meetings is to get involved in your own healing. You will find other men and women who are struggling with the same pain as you. You will discover that the first step in coming to grips with a depression that won't quit is for you to surrender it, quit fighting it. Let the God as you understand it take over your life and help let it restore you to sanity, peace and understanding of the way in which you can find the path out of your prison of depression. *Depressed Anonymous* works if you begin the work of the spiritual programme that we are going to outline in this book. Depression is a moral problem and as such there needs to be a moral solution, one part of which is to admit that we are responsible for ourselves and that we can't blame it on genes, psychological predispositions or one's spouse. We are going to take charge. We choose to undepress ourselves. Today! One day at a time!

In the past we have found that the programme works if you keep at it. The best way to keep at it is to attend meetings as often as you can, so that you are able to hear how others have got out of their depression and are learning how to stay in touch with their Higher Power. You know there is simply something positive being part of a self-help group and being able to talk about what you are feeling. You do have a choice though, and as Abraham Lincoln was supposed to have said, "You are about as happy as you make up your mind to be." I agree with that. But let me warn you – it isn't easy to do something different from what you have been doing most of your life. That is especially true when it comes to the way we see ourselves, the world and others. There are no magic pills and no easy answers to bring us immediately out of this inner pain and anguish. It does take time and work.

If you really want to leave behind your painful sadness, the daily tears and the feelings of worthlessness, then begin now to admit the unmanageableness of your depression. You have had it with feeling out of control!

That's the way it is with depression – over the years you get comfortable with feeling miserable, which doesn't mean you like it but that you're just too afraid to risk feeling something different. When you want to change and leave your depression behind the choice that you want to make is immediately dashed to the ground because you just feel that there is no hope for you. "I can't pull myself up by my bootstraps and start to feel better", you tell yourself. Most of the time we tell ourselves that we'll do it when we feel better. Folks, let me tell you something – you'll never feel better until you begin physically to get moving! We all know that we feel better only when we get into gear and get busy – distracting ourselves from those ever-present miserable thoughts whispering how bad we are and how hopeless life seems to be.

You have to admit that you're powerless over this depressed behaviour and likewise admit that your life is unmanageable. You don't want to go on living this way. In fact, some days you feel that you just want to lie down and die, but deep inside you there is that Spirit, call it God, Higher Power, or whatever, that keeps you searching for a way out. A part of you is still hanging on and giving you hope to try to live through this pain of hopelessness and isolation. You just know there has got to be something out there that will give you at least a glimmer of hope. This part of you has been competing for years with those other parts of you that say, "End it all", "Give up – you'll never feel better", or worse, "You are losing your mind and you can't go through all this for another day."

But listen to that small voice, folks – this is the voice that has been trying to be heard for years, only other negative voices and our own old negative mental tapes have had more training in getting their message across. **Now that small voice, that little part of you that wants to have light and some hope is getting up the courage to ask more for itself.** It tries to get stronger as it attempts to outshine those other parts of ourselves; those parts that have been telling us how trapped we are in our feelings of worthlessness. How often do people say that part of them wants to do this and yet another part of them wants to do that. I believe that is the best expression of the conflict that goes on in many of us when we are depressed. Usually the part that is hurting and sad speaks the loudest and so often gets the most attention – but why not, it's hurting. When that part of us gets hurt it wants to withdraw – to hide and cry. It's like a small child who wants to run away from all the anguish and disappointment. But inside of us when the parts are struggling with each other it's like two teams pulling in a tug of war, and that takes energy to keep alive. We get worn out as we continually ruminate about how sad we are feeling and how hopeless everything looks. Most days we just want to go to our room, lie down and sleep. Have you noticed that the more depressed you become the more sleep you need? Or don't need? There is that constant jittery feeling that won't go away and which ever reminds us of the hollowness of our lives. The life we live is as bitter as ashes in our mouths.

Let's listen now to the long-denied part of us that speaks out in favour of a change – that voice of hope that says we will feel cheerful one day. The small part of us that says that we should risk going to this meeting and admit that yes, I am depressed, and yes, I am going to find my way out of this prison by taking stock of my strengths and by beginning to want to hope. You do have a choice. You can begin to let go of your fears of what life will be like without this constant, gnawing feeling inside of you that produces that awful jitteriness. You will find lots of acceptance from the group as you listen to the many ways others like yourself have surrendered their problems to their Higher Power and have begun to find a peace and sanity that they never thought existed. The old tapes in your head will whisper that there is no hope for you, that no one is as badly off as you are, and that nobody will want to help you as you don't deserve anything anyway. Often these old tapes have been with us since childhood and many of our adult depressions have their roots in our childhood. Many people do not remember much of their childhood, but repressing memories does not mean that the emotions belonging to these experiences in childhood disappear.

Depression is a sign of a lost and ungrieved childhood (11,14). Many times our depression stems from a shame, a feeling sad about something that happened to us a long time ago and which has been blocked from our memories because it was at the time too painful to look at. We felt ashamed. We even might have felt that we were a mistake, that we have no right to exist. It still is making us sad.

We can only live now, and so we have to let go of past hurts and past resentments. We can learn that it's OK to tell others what we feel, that we feel bad, that we have given up all hope and that we have tried to do away with our own lives. The group, you will discover, accepts your statements of despair, as they have experienced the very same feelings. You will find acceptance, encouragement and new skills as you begin to form new friendships and slowly begin to believe that maybe you too can feel better with a little time and work. You begin to live with more hope as you hear each member express their feelings of how their life was before DA and how it is now as they practise the twelve-step programme in their daily lives.

Depressed Anonymous means hope – as long as you want to get out of the pit of depression just start to believe that little voice which says, "Yes, I am hopeful, I will feel better too. The other members of *Depressed Anonymous* give me hope. Others have made it out of the deep lonely pit of depression and so can I. I choose to be happy even if I don't feel happy right away. I am going to risk feeling different from this wretched sadness that I feel all the time. I have nothing to lose – except my fear of the future."

But with our new way of living and thinking we are going to stay in the now. We know tomorrow produces anxiety and fear. Yesterday is there with all the old past hurts and anger. All I have is the *now*! If I live in the now I can begin to try to stay out of yesterday, with all its old wounds and hurts, and resist living in tomorrow with its unknown problems. Negative thoughts about our past or those about tomorrow can numb our feelings so that we don't have to feel the pain of whatever it is that isolates us from the world around us. We also admit, like any one person addicted to a person, place, thing, chemical or drug, that our lives are out of control. We have to admit that by depressing ourselves we have chosen sadding ourselves as our drug of choice. We medicate ourselves with sadness any time we might have to change the way we live our lives. Sometimes our depression/sadness arises out of guilt as we continue to turn our personal mistakes into giant catastrophes – this continues to make us feel we're nothing and valueless. This all adds to our frustration and the feeling of our being out of control.

We know that if we just give up our struggle against depression and admit our powerlessness over it we can begin to surrender it to our Higher Power and practise letting go of it. I can decide that I want to feel good again. I can decide that I want to feel happy and put this constant sadness and hollowness behind me once and for all. I know that no longer will I have to retreat or flee from these sad feelings and escape with sleep, overactivity or drugs. I know that, whenever my sadness seems unending, I then just admit that I am not helpless and that I can do something about it because I have the tools and I can learn the skills that I didn't know were available to me before. Now I am deciding to think, act and behave differently, much to my personal credit and a new-found trust in a Higher Power. I am a sailor who sees the land, knows the right direction and does the rowing to get where I want to get. The twelve steps are my compass. I also know that this group of people which we call DA will help me assume a sense of no longer feeling out of control. Instead I believe I will begin to take responsibility for my life and risk getting better. In time I can trust the group with my story and my struggles against the heaviness of daily life. In time I can trust God to take away my hurts and pains and sadness, just as I have begun to trust the members of DA with my deepest hurts and feelings of loneliness.

This first step is really the most important step in that we admit that our lives are out of control – that our lives are unmanageable – that we need to believe that we now have to make a choice for our own happiness. We can continue to dwell in the mire, the self-pity of depression, or we can begin to work with others and see that there is hope for our depression.

The starting point is the admission that so far everything we have tried has not worked. How often have I heard members of DA say that since coming to DA their lives have become less sad and they feel more hopeful. Some of them have reduced their antidepressant medication, and have had their doctors get them off the medication altogether. I believe the proof is in watching the person in the programme who, week after week, gradually begins to show improvement. All improvement comes slowly – thank God for that or we couldn't handle it! I have noticed that people who continually work their programme and surrender to the Higher Power begin to look different – that's right, they look different. They begin to seem more relaxed and their faces begin to assume a softness – a new radiance. I can tell that they are getting better, and the group lets them know how much better they look. It's good to get positive feedback that we are doing something right.

The God that we know speaks to us through members of the DA group. The Higher Power will put a new sense of purpose into your life once you know how to turn to it and surrender your pain. The DA will lead you safely and gently! The miracle is in the group.

One of the things that we try to keep from happening in the group is to have people label themselves as "depressives", as if that's what their total being is all about. No, we are more than just people who are experiencing depression, we are also people who are working on this sadness in ourselves and we continue to surrender it to the Higher Power or God as we understand Him. To say that we are "a depressive" is like a woman who says that she is just "a housewife", as if this particular role makes her all that she is. Also, sometimes the recovering alcoholic says he or she is just an alcoholic; no, they are more than an alcoholic. We never want to have a single kind of behaviour limit who we are – or define our identity. We are more than any one behaviour, even though that one might influence the rest of our behaviour. Once we admit that our depressed thinking is what conditions us to see our world as a hopeless place to live, the more we will try to change the way we think. What we want to accomplish in DA is to listen to those folks who are working their programme, who experience a new sense of control over their feelings and appreciate and learn new skills that help them from going into the depths of depression once again.

Some people say that once a person gets undepressed that should help them no longer need the meetings and fellowship of the group – but that's like telling the alcoholic he/she can drink again after so many weeks of AA and working the twelve steps. This is where the addictions have so much in common with each other. Addictions all have the same characteristic in that they are used so as to allow an individual to escape a painful reality or stressful experience. Another addiction is smoking, and it is used to help people cope with stressful situations. I also see overeating as an addiction because it helps people stuff the pain and emptiness which they find in their lives. In like manner depression can be used as an escape from the reality of living a life filled with uncertainty and risk. No wonder depression is such a hellish experience because it is always the same, and the people who are severely depressed have convinced themselves with their circular way of thinking that life will never get better and that they are doomed to this sadness with its continual hurt and pain. You only can hope when there is uncertainty and unpredictability in one's life. With depression one is faced with a hell of isolated sadness. But this is where the first step comes into play for all of us who have been depressed and who are struggling to free ourselves from its grip. We are hooked on an addictive behaviour and a habitual way of thinking when we continue to depress ourselves – we have opted for the belief that this fleeing into sadness is the only way to live our lives. Could we say that we are *sad*dicts? Withdrawal into addictive behaviour and thinking is what keeps us from facing the reality of living a life filled with hope and peace.

Like with any addictive behaviour, we have to continue to focus on ourselves and the ways to stay spiritually connected with God's will for us as we go about our daily lives. There must be a continued practising of the twelve steps, as they are the force that keeps us ever alert from falling back into all the old ways of thinking and acting, which cause us to remain sad and keep us from having to make the choice of being happy. Just as the people who are addicted to gambling, eating, alcohol or depression follow the twelve steps and take to heart the need for a continual turning of their lives over to the Higher Power for wisdom, guidance and serenity, so does the person who is an active member of DA. The DA member has no reason to fear talking out with members of the group his or her need to use sad and defeating thinking to punish themselves for being so worthless and bad.

One of the more constant behaviours of the individual depressing is to engage in fewer and fewer pleasant activities. The person depressed just can't bring himself or herself to do anything that might cause a sense of elation or pleasure. If you feel that you are bad, worthless and without any value then you can't get yourself to do something that might make you have a good feeling about yourself. An individual depressing can make himself or herself feel anxious, sick and even faint. With the support of a group like DA one can begin to see that life doesn't have to be lived alone in agony or misery, and that is precisely the miracle of the group. You begin to see that you can stay parked in neutral in your misery and feel hopeless, or you can step out in faith, as most members of the group do, and admit that you've had it with this sadness and begin to choose life. I do believe a renewed sense of hope is in our hands – we can choose to be sad or we can choose to live with purposeful joy. It's a risk we choose to take.

I remember a client who once told me that he was afraid to come to DA because he imagined everyone there was probably filled with self-pity and had sad tales to tell – why depress yourself more? he asked. I suggested that Ralph go and try a couple of meetings before he gave his negative verdict on the group. He went to a meeting, expressed his feelings of surprise that they had said aloud what he felt, and went back time and again until he felt he was in a position to take control over his life once again. He said that it was the first time he could go to a place where everyone accepted him for what he was, and they didn't say that he was crazy or losing his mind as he shared his experience of depression. He knew as well as I did that depression can cause one to lose the ability to concentrate as well as to remember things. It's a secure feeling to hear that someone else has had the same experience as your own. Going to a DA meeting when you're depressing is like going to a foreign country and finding someone who speaks your language. When you speak depression the group knows the language.

This is the first step – surrender and admit that your depression has made your life unmanageable and miserable. Acknowledge that your life is indeed unmanageable and proceed onto the next step, where you know that you don't have it in your will power to turn it around but that only the Higher Power of God as you understand Him can remove your sadness and despair. You have the choice! Make a decision to want to feel better – today!

Bill's Story

I became an active member of DA after seeing Hugh for three or four months. I never knew I was depressed. I never understood. I knew that I needed to make changes in my life. Many depressives have this trouble, namely, not being able to admit that something is truly, truly wrong in their lives and that they need to change.

I started to realize that I was depressed seven or eight years ago. It started after the breakup with a girlfriend. I was devastated. I had good friends at work, I am well educated, with two degrees after my name, but I wasn't fulfilled. My world was falling apart. I lost a job and then another job, and I lost my girl. I wanted to be left alone. The burden was too unreal. I didn't want to get up in the morning. I just wanted to be left alone to be isolated and bored. It was tough. I was nasty and mean. I sometimes still behave like this. I get angry and I get frustrated and get upset with myself.

Thank God for the girl who said that I didn't like myself and that I should go for counselling. Without her ever telling me that, I would never have changed. Hugh, the counsellor, told me that motivation follows action.

Before DA I was paralysed, I couldn't even interview for a job, I had no confidence. I could hardly get out of bed of a morning. I would just mope around and never really get moving. I would pick fights with my mother. I didn't know what to do with my anger or frustration, I didn't know where to place my misguided fears.

But then I found a place, the DA group, *Depressed Anonymous*. We were a small group at first in Louisville, Kentucky. In this group, we all had a story, and we had to let it out. I thought that no one could be in as bad a shape as I was in. Everyone, I thought, was perfectly happy. We started the DA group about a year ago. We took one step at a time, one step a week for twelve weeks. As time went on, we began to share more about ourselves, the good and the bad. We shared one step at a time.

Being depressed is like being in a deep dark hole with no one to turn to. Your friends don't understand you, people around you don't understand your mood changes. I was so lonely that I didn't know what to do about myself. I just didn't give a damn. But now my self-esteem is up. Finally I believe in myself. DA has given me all that back. My attitude is positive. Right now I feel as if I am in recovery. I still go to the group because without the group I get argumentative, and with the group I keep on an even keel.

DA is a spiritual journey, which makes you go back into your past, find the rubbish there, and let it go. Without the DA group or a group like it, I don't think I could function in the world as I know it. I thank God for the people who have the courage to come to the group. They will grow and learn. There is no easy way out. You don't change overnight. You have just got to keep working at it. I have been in the trenches with nowhere to go. I find this very common in us humans. Change is very tough for us. We would rather bear so much pain before we are willing to change. This black hole is a terrible thing. I wish no one would ever feel it. It is painful and nasty.

This is my short story. I was down and I was out. I really couldn't care, at one time, if I lived or died, but now I do. It really didn't matter. I met a great girl and decided to get married. I couldn't have done it without DA. It's a wonderful experience. I'm learning how to take care of myself. I met a lot of new friends at DA. It takes time to change. You've got to be willing to take time to change. It might not work for everyone. But without DA I wouldn't be where I am today.

Step Two

Came to Believe that a Power greater than Ourselves could restore Us to Sanity

What do we consider to be the Higher Power or the God that is larger and more powerful than our personal depression? In our prayer we believe that God or the Higher Power can free us from the burden of our joylessness, and that the why of our depression is not so important as the fact that we are depressed. What is it about our complete dependence on this obsession with sadness, our chronic fatigue and feelings of worthlessness that won't let go of us? Granted, sometimes we feel depression is a comfort, and we're afraid to let go of it because we don't as yet know what will replace it. Hope tends to be unpredictable whereas the pain of depression is constant and predictable. We can depend on it.

We have given ourselves over to the belief that this growing feeling of helplessness is what must govern our lives, moods and behaviour. We have given it licence to run roughshod over every part of our life and over our relationships. Most people can't see inside us and discover the pain that makes up our every waking moment. For the most part we are able to hide how miserable we feel.

Our awareness is constantly shifting inside ourselves to monitor our every mood as it shifts from anxiety to fear, from anger to rage and back to sadness – our sadness and helplessness make us feel angry about how boxed in we always feel. All parts of us in pain cry out for attention.

We learn that there is a God who is supposed to love us and take care of us, but we are afraid to let go of who we believe we are or what we feel we have to be. Trust is something that we have given up a long time ago. Trust is hard for us, especially when we that feel life, people and our circumstances have completely let us down. For so long now unpleasant feelings have led us to believe that we have no right to happiness, now or in the future. We have grown up with a sense of suspicion of those around us who appear happy and satisfied with life. Instead we find it safer to back away from too much involvement with other people, because they would see how bad we really are if they got to know us and then our secret would be out. We don't ever know what "normal" feels like because we constantly feel so hollow and empty inside.

We now know that once we have taken that first step and admitted we are powerless because of our depression we can let go of this constant companion, this ever-present depression, and simply believe that our God, as we understand Him to be, will restore us to serenity.

Our addiction to turning inside ourselves and feeling sad is just one other way to deny our true situation. In reality, we have become *sadd*icts! Whenever we want to be comforted we turn to this feeling of powerlessness which continues to validate our sense of worthlessness.

If we want to continue feeling that we are no good, bad and worthless, this type of negative thinking can do nothing but produce the self-fulfilling prophecy, namely, that we will never feel good. When we begin to look at our strengths, listen to other people who were once depressed, we can begin to see a glimmer of light and hope coming along our path. We also can begin to believe this Force, Higher Power, God is asking us to give hope a chance in our despairing lives. We begin to hear the older members of the *Depressed Anonymous* group share how they began to put their trust in something bigger than themselves and were ready to move out of the pain of their small, painful worlds and begin to grow. This power that is greater than ourselves could be members of the DA group, a book, Jesus, or whatever a person wants to make it. Most persons working the twelve steps, for whatever addiction or co-dependency, admit that it is their dependence on the Higher Power that keeps them sober, serene and balanced. As their trust level goes up so does their mood.

It's an addiction if you find yourself continually bashing yourself for past mistakes and/or failures. It is this constant rumination that puts us in the negative spiral which leads to more isolation, withdrawal and psychic pain. The familiar feeling of sadness and the continual inner hollowness that make our life so miserable becomes our security.

Often when we are closely intertwined with some compulsive/addictive behaviour, it isn't until we let go of the pain that drives our depression that the original pain, hurt, guilt or shame gradually melts away. In the group meeting each of us begins our new directions by listening to older twelve-step people who speak openly and honestly about the time when *they* were so depressed that they couldn't even get out of bed in the morning, or were so tired that they could hardly wait to go to bed and sleep away their unending misery. Some people have a difficult time trusting those people who work their programme and who say that they would feel better if they continue to attend meetings, work their twelve-step programme, eat properly, get an exercise programme and talk about their sadness with others. They keep themselves imprisoned in their depression by continually repeating to themselves that since nothing has worked in the past why should something good happen now?

At each DA meeting we hear different members of the group tell how their Higher Power helped return them to a peace, a serenity that they had never experienced until they starting coming to *Depressed Anonymous* and began working on themselves. Now they can spend time in prayer and meditation with the Higher Power guiding their lives through the times of darkness. In time they have found giving up their depression to the care of the Higher Power almost a pleasure. It is our belief that if we want to begin to live, we must surrender our addiction to depression. The more we are tempted to seek comfort and bash ourselves with thoughts of how bad we are, the more depressed we become. But on the positive side the more we begin to take mastery over our thinking and our listless behaviour, the more small, gradual gains we will make in seeing some light at the end of the tunnel. By living just for today, that is, one day at a time, and not in the hurts and anger of yesterday or the fear and anxiety of tomorrow, we will begin to see a spark of light coming over the horizon.

Look around at the group and listen to the stories of how they are feeling better and doing better by just keeping their lives simple and less cluttered. The persons who begin to leave the prison of depression are the ones who desire a change and are taking the appropriate steps to gain their freedom. Ever since they came into the group they have heard how one person after another had been helped by their belief that a power greater than themselves can restore them to some sort of serenity and peace.

Dorothy Rowe says that some depressed people wish to be a martyr and give a thousand and one reasons why they should stay depressed (17, 23). They can think up thousands of painful thoughts about how bad they are and how they don't deserve the cheer and joy that most of us frequently experience in our daily lives. Some run over and over again in their minds the awful things that they have done, and become used to their continual ruminating over their own sense of worthlessness. They have fallen into the depressed person's morbid need to feel bad. The sadness continues to eat away at the very heart of the person until there is no more hope and the light at the end of the tunnel has been snuffed out. In their hopelessness of ever getting better they throw away the only key that will unlock their prison, and that is the key called **hope**. Getting to the hope is at the heart of getting our lives and feelings reorganized. We begin to believe that maybe I too can overcome my depression like other members of the group. Not only am I consciously changing the way I think but likewise I am forcing myself to get involved with the other members of the group and am making friends. I know that withdrawing from others is one of the first signs that we are depressing ourselves. But it is in the continual contact with others like myself that I can begin to find a way out of my depression.

If all I can believe in is my own sense of feeling inadequate or worthless then it is time to look for something positive to believe in. We come to believe that there is another way out of this hell which we experience as sadness and emptiness. Once we make a commitment to change the way we think, behave, feel and interact with others, the more we will want to ask the Higher Power for help along our way of recovery. So often in the past we have been so self-reliant that God or the Higher Power didn't have room to move in our lives. We are ever mindful that this change takes time but in reality we can only live one day at a time. We have to believe that this Power will gradually allow us to feel and act differently, and by that I mean it will allow us to act with hope. The more that we trust ourselves to feel hopeful the greater is the possibility that our depression will pass. We know that our feeling sad is related to our thinking sad thoughts, and many times we aren't even conscious why we are feeling sad and down.

The group helps us share with each other our feelings of isolation, and the members support our small but gradual steps toward improvement in our mood. DA is a group which addresses itself solely to depression and the group's success as a group comes honestly. We say who we are and make no apologies. We know that when we share with the others our story of depression they know what we are talking about because they have been there. The group doesn't sugarcoat the task of turning our depressive lifestyle around. Most people, including our family and close friends, want to tell us to snap out of our depression, as though we can just turn the feelings of sadness and hopelessness on and off like a tap. The key again is to admit first of all that we are depressed and then believe that the Higher Power can restore us to sanity.

The sanity of the twelve-step programme is what will eventually help you change how you look at yourself and

your experience of depression. The programme shows
that just because you have always felt miserable is no
reason to remain miserable for the rest of your life. The
sanity of placing your trust in a Power greater than yourself opens up great possibilities for your personal happiness and success. If you have felt you had to be in total
control of every situation in your life and that you somehow couldn't allow yourself to feel half-way good about
yourself, then coming to believe in a power greater than
yourself might be a frightening experience. What would
happen if suddenly you couldn't control your unhappy
situation with the comfort of sadness or self-pity? Haven't
our sadness and thoughts of unworthiness been our last
refuge from having to face ourselves, take charge and
accept responsibility for our own lives? For many, just
knowing that they might have a choice and be able to
choose to feel differently can be a startling revelation. I
can choose to be happy or I can choose to stay feeling
miserable.

The escape into feelings of worthlessness and resig-
nation over my depressing feelings is no longer an acceptable way for me to delay the hard choice of being responsible for me. This statement is not made to make you feel
guilty but only to help you see that, with time and by
working the twelve steps on a daily basis and having the
ongoing fellowship and support of the *Depressed Anonymous* group, you can begin to choose a way out.

We have a new way of looking at ourselves in *Depressed
Anonymous*. We believe that if I am to feel better and get
through this painful experience I call depression then I
am going to have to surrender some parts of myself that
have become like old friends – old friends of the negative
and toxic sort. These parts tell me that I am bad, worthless
and unable to be happy. You have made these irrational

and negative voices the force to live by. Now *Depressed Anonymous* asks you in the second step to begin to make a mental assent to the fact that only a Power greater than yourself can free you from the prison of depression. This power will help you let go of your self-doubts, irrational beliefs and negative self-image. Granted, we want to tell you that change is never easy but only possible when you choose to place your trust in the Higher Power. The miracle of the group is that it will show you that you are important, that you will be accepted and that you will learn how others in the group with the same experience of depression as your own are now experiencing hope.

This new belief in the Higher Power is not the creation of any organized religion but instead is the Power that creates the universe. Our surrender and trust in it frees it to work its way in our lives. That is the paradox of the twelve steps – the more we depend on the Higher Power instead of our addictions, the more free we in reality become.

This new belief will in time give us the power to think about risking life without having to be dead sure of what the next moment will bring. It appears that when we are depressed we are so sure that since everything in the past has been bad so should everything be in the future. You just expect everything to turn out badly. So, the tomorrows never look very good to us. We need therefore to live in the NOW and it is when we surrender to the Higher Power that we finally begin to feel a safety never felt before.

We also know that our withdrawal from others has given excessive power to those already entrenched feelings of worthlessness and sadness. It seems that our inactivity and social isolation just help build higher and stronger walls to our prison. This is why we need to hear

stories like Bob's, who was one of the original members
of *Depressed Anonymous* – he felt that DA was one of the
few places where he could laugh, where he could be
himself. He was with people who understood him and
they didn't consider him crazy or reinforce his own feelings that he might be losing his mind.

Jane was given an ultimatum to get help by her daughter,
who saw the *Depressed Anonymous* group as a last chance
for her mother, who was suicidal and despondent over
the death of her husband a few months earlier. Jane didn't
want to come to the meeting; she came only to please her
daughter.

She watched everyone at her first meeting and when
she saw that they weren't too weird she finally thought
she'd throw her story at them toward the end of the
meeting. To her surprise no one fell out of their seats.
She felt sure that the shock of saying that she'd tried to
kill herself twice without success would surely get a rise
out of the group – instead it got people to share their
own hard times, and they also shared how the group
has continued to help them through hard times. They
suggested that Jane keep coming back to the group, and
encouraged her with the belief that she would continue
to feel better following each meeting.

Jane did keep coming back to the meetings, and she
started to look different as her face began to soften and
she had a twinkle in her eye as she came to the meetings
wanting to give instead of just receive. Now with the
support of the group she has begun to take charge of her
life and is an active member, continually telling others
how it was and how it is now, now that she is on the
road to recovery. Jane found no comments such as that
she should "snap out of" her depression, or that she was

losing her mind or that she was suffering from some mental illness. Instead, at each meeting she found people of intelligence who accepted her recovery. Members of a group also gently confront each other when the need arises, with the sole motive of helping people see themselves as others see them.

Jane accepted her powerlessness and gave it to God as she understood this newly found Power and discovered that the grace of God could do for her what she could never have done on her own.

Alcoholics Anonymous (1) tells us: We never apologize to anyone for depending upon our Creator. We can laugh at those who think spirituality the way of weakness. Paradoxically, it is the way of strength. The verdict of the ages is that faith means courage. All men (women) of faith have courage. They trust their God. Instead, we let him demonstrate, through us, what he can do. We ask him to remove our fear and direct our attention to what he would have us be. At once, we commence to outgrow fear.

Fear is at the centre of our depression and as such has to be removed if we are to progress along our way to recovery. With courage and trust in the Higher Power you cannot fail as you continue to work this twelve-step programme. There is a saying that I think fits most of us in recovery and that is this: *The truth will set you free; but first it will make you miserable*. What it means is that if you really want to start feeling better and differently we will have to confess to our need to make amends to ourselves and to others, and begin the process of choosing life over depression.

Bill W., a co-founder of Alcoholics Anonymous, wrote:

Our first woman alcoholic had been a patient of Dr Harry Tiebout's, and he had handed her a prepublication manuscript copy of the Big Book. The first reading made her rebellious, but the second convinced her. Presently she came to a meeting held in our living room, and from there she returned to the sanatorium carrying this classic message to a fellow patient: "We aren't alone any more." (2)

No longer will anyone who has ever been treated for depression and who feels a need for understanding and ongoing support ever be alone again as long as *Depressed Anonymous* is around. It is by being part of the group that you will experience that miracle of the group which is to find that a Power greater than yourself is about to restore you to a feeling of serenity and personal hope.

Step Three

Made a Decision to turn our Will and our Lives over to the *Care of God As We Understood Him*

This decision to turn our lives over to God is one of the most important we will ever make in our lives. The more we surrender to His peace the more we will find our way. It is the paradox of our existence that it is in the letting go that we receive, and it is only in being in God's will as we understand Him that we can have real life and joy. "The spiritual life is not a theory. WE HAVE TO LIVE IT" (1).

God's will is hard to determine at times – especially at such critical times as now when we want to give up on ourselves. This is the time to give up our will and say "God, you take it – I've had it! You do the leading now!" And you know, God will. You will begin to get more honest with yourself as you begin to look a little more closely at why you have been sad most of your life. And I might add here that for many of the members of *Depressed Anonymous* they seem to have been depressed from the moment of their conception. Even though many people come to *Depressed Anonymous* to help them through times of significant loss in their life, such as the death of a spouse, the breakup of a relationship, the loss of a job or loss of self-esteem, many others are attempting to relearn how to act more wisely and treat themselves kindly. Depressed people don't know how to have fun or even how to plan a pleasant activity – it's completely out of their experience. They spend most of their time berating themselves for all their real or imagined mistakes in their lives.

DA helps us feel that we are beginning to have some mastery over our lives. Because of mastery over how we talk to ourselves we find that our mood begins to change and life seems more hopeful and satisfying. One thing we need to remember is that thoughts produce moods and moods produce feelings and feelings produce behaviour. If we can begin to think more positively about our lives and less about how bad we are, and how we no longer have to be perfect, then we will begin to feel how much happier our lives can be. We will also relearn how to trust our feelings, as we trust God more to let Him thaw out our frozen feelings.

By a daily prayer and meditation time we soon learn that the more frequent our contact is with the Higher Power, the more in touch this force will be in our lives and the more trust will you give to its leading. Once you have had more cheerful days than sad days you will begin to see what in actuality has brought you down in the past. These sad thoughts will appear as red flags that will warn you to turn your negative thoughts to some positive picture and imagine yourself in a positive situation. You will learn how this can change your mood around. You can change your mood by changing the way you think. Thinking causes moods which cause behaviour. Meditation is likewise a waiting upon the Higher Power to reveal itself in our lives. We try daily to make conscious contact with the God of our lives as we understand Him. We begin to love ourselves and each other, and when we attend our meetings we learn that it is in our openness to the Higher Power that this God of our understanding can operate. Our lives begin to assume a new hopefulness.

You are fortunate to be in DA and can be grateful as you hear stories of people like yourself who are willing to come together and support each other in their efforts to find hope and peace.

Depressed Anonymous is a place to clean house, forgive ourselves and others, and begin to depend on God as we understand Him. We need to develop a God-consciousness. We learn about God from books but most importantly through our own personal experience. We experience God and the Higher Power in our group and during our personal prayer and meditation time. We come together at DA and all our sessions begin and end with prayer. Our programme is a spiritual one. We are not a religion with set dogmas and doctrines but we are searchers of our true selves where we intend to find God and surrender our will to Him. This small step can lead us to greater healing and hope.

Jim, for instance, learned that he needed more "SUN-SPOTS" to bask himself in. These "SUNSPOTS" are meditation times where we can focus on all those pleasurable events, people, places or things that can make us feel happy. The trouble with most of us when we are depressed is that our whole life seems to go on in a deep pit with the eighty-foot hole and the eight-foot ladder.

One good way to escape from this prison is to get with a group of people who, by joining each other's section of the ladder, will all eventually get to the top and out of this deep dark hole that we call depression. Think upon these small "SUNSPOTS" throughout the day and know that you are gradually coming into the light of a new day. Prepare a list of memories which at one time in your life were the cause of some joy or pleasure, and try to recreate that activity in your imagination as often as you can. At first all you might be able to do is just make a mental decision to do it even though at the time you don't feel any particular pleasant emotion. Keep at it and with the continued encouragement of the group you will be able to recapture a little joy and peace. You will begin to have more mastery over your life and the world and this in itself can lower your feelings of sadness. When you have a negative image or thought which produces an unpleasant feeling replace it immediately with three positive and pleasant thoughts or mental images. In DA we call this THE LAW OF THE THREES. One negative thought is immediately replaced by three pleasant thoughts and/or memories.

For the depressed person, giving up old ways of thinking and acting is much like giving up any other addiction – at first letting go of the old behaviour makes us feel uncomfortable. The old behaviour wants to cling to our spirit like swamp mud hangs on to knee-high boots. Before your participation in DA you would go home from work, get by yourself and ruminate on how bad you felt. This new behaviour will help you think differently about yourself. You will find that this Higher Power, or God as you understand Him, is not the same God that you might have met when you were young. When you were a child you came to believe that God was watching you, ready to punish you if you were not perfect. You will begin to develop an adult and new way of being related to God as you understand Him. With time, persistence and patience you will gradually trust your life to this Higher Power.

One thing the Higher Power accomplishes for any of us is the freedom of being in His will. By turning your life and will over to the Higher Power you can make a new beginning, you get a new start, you can forgive yourself for all the times you thought you needed to be perfect, and instead accept your own self and imagine yourself the happy person you want to be. And if you attend meetings regularly and become involved you will begin to feel better about yourself, your world and your future.

I promise you that as you continue to learn to trust others and feel accepted by them your face will soften and you will be more relaxed knowing that you are OK. Members of the group will support you every inch of the way. Your *hope* will return in good measure the more you attend meetings. You will begin to feel renewed as you learn how not to be sad, how not to feel guilty and ashamed because you feel you are not like other people. Now instead of thinking about the beautiful persons, relationships or a part of the self that you may have lost, you set goals every day of how you are going to lick this depression once and for all. You have no doubt that you want to feel better and you just know God is with you. I hope that because of your own understanding of the experience of depression and what damage it can do to people, you will now want to be used by God to reach out to others and help them regain their self-esteem and confidence. People depressed don't look on themselves too kindly.

We all believe the saying that "Motivation follows action". We all have heard it said, and we have said it ourselves, that "I will do it when I feel better!" We never feel better and so we never start to change the way we feel, think and act. The feeling of helplessness remains.

The decision to begin to turn our lives and will over to God as we understand Him can only work for us as we learn to let go and let the Higher Power work its will in our lives and minds.

Being in God's will is the beginning of peace and the beginning of the end of your depression with its hollowness and jitters!

We are talking about spirituality here – we are not proclaiming a religion. This is the difference of great importance. We are not subject to a book of dogmas, theological treatises or doctrine made by human beings. We are advocating a spirituality that puts God first in our lives and lets Him run our lives as He sees fit. When we talk about surrendering we get scared. How many people have I heard say, "I don't know if I want to give up my will – what will happen to me then?" This is an honest question and one that I had asked myself many times. But it was only after I hit bottom and found my depression too much for me to handle that I knew I had to give up my way of doing things, for my life couldn't get any worse. It's when we feel we can't go on with our own life that we get in touch with the waiting and loving and ever-present Higher Power. It's easy to say I want to give up my will – just to say the words "I surrender" – and that is a good start, but the temptation to go back to our sadness, to sad ourselves, is a constant one in the beginning days of our recovery.

Control is an issue which all addicts of whatever substance, emotion or relationships have to look at sooner or later in their recovery. Removing the need to be in control can only be got at by being willing to give it up to someone else – for us in DA that means the Higher Power. When I can admit that my depression has become unmanageable it is only at this point that I can begin to gain control over it and begin to live with hope and joy.

In DA we are exposed constantly to the tough message that we have to give up our self-pity and sadness if we want to be happy. We have to think in terms of what is possible with God in our lives. Sometimes people come to DA and don't want to talk about God or the twelve steps, and can't understand what this has to do with how bad they feel. If after a number of meetings they still don't want to work the twelve steps we recommend other groups for them. DA is a spiritual programme and it is allowing the Higher Power into our lives that eventually delivers us from the habit of feeling sad and depressed. We in DA are committed to working the twelve steps and listening to each other share how God as we understand Him has worked in our lives.

Daily we pray that God will release us from our depression and that He will show us His will and His way to peace. Don't give up on yourself but come back to meetings week after week. In time the truth about yourself as revealed to you by the group and the Higher Power will set you free. That is a promise!

One of the major areas of our lives that we have a difficult time with is getting in touch with our feelings. Many of us who are presently depressed know that one of our great defences is the denial of our feelings – our ability to feel is diminished as we continually choose numbness over vitality.

Jim was a member of a DA group and he would come to each meeting and just say his name and that was that. Of course we all try to accept people where they are and when they first come to DA we let them know that it is

OK just to sit and listen and learn from the other members of the group. Everyone realizes that you never have to speak at a meeting but that you always have the right to pass and remain silent.

Jim came with a deep anger and mistrust of professionals, especially doctors, counsellors and psychiatrists, whom he said were more interested in money than in helping people. Jim also felt overwhelmed by all the things he had to attend to in his life and was angry at the cards life dealt out to him.

The DA group in their own inimitable fashion shared with him how each had found some peace and joy by making daily a good effort in working the twelve steps and turning their lives over to God or the Higher Power. They each expressed their own struggles and shared how coming back to the group week after week started them back on the road to recovery. They were feeling so bad that they had to trust someone with how bad they felt and so they came to the group that said it was there for depressed people. And when they started to hear how other persons were able to trust each other with their own pain, hurt, guilt and shame it wasn't long before they progressed to the third step and were able to trust the Higher Power with their lives. The group members all expressed to Jim how they each had made a mental decision to turn their lives and their depression over to the Higher Power because they had no place to go but up. It was this surrendering to the Higher Power or God as we understand Him that was the beginning of the overcoming of some people's addiction to the comfort of their depression. They now are willing and ready to live with some hope. In time Jim got in touch with his anger, shared it with people who accepted it, and so was able gradually to move out of the shell that kept him from the hope that life would ever be any different for him. The depressed person just believes and takes it on faith that he/she will always be depressed and sad. Now that negative belief of being depressed forever has to be reframed and we have to tell ourselves that if we have a positive faith our life will be better and we will begin to see changes. Many times we get what we choose when it comes to our personal feelings.

Jim also felt that his whole problem was a chemical imbalance and that he really wasn't responsible for his plight of continual sadness. But the members of the group pointed out that any emotion, especially a negative one, will in time have certain physiological consequences which can cause the human body to get fatigued, change the appetite, cause sleep problems and promote a general feeling of helplessness. Even though antidepressants are fine for the time when they are needed to lift one's mood, one doesn't want to depend on them over any long period of time. Most doctors are sensitive to this fact and will recommend their patients to see a counsellor or psychologist while the medication, they hope, begins to lift the mood of the patient. Many people find that by taking some medication they can work and function fairly normally and feel able to confront their sadness, perhaps by talking to a therapist, or friend, or with their DA group.

With any addiction to an experience, be it alcohol, eating, gambling, smoking, and for us depression, we all know that there is no "cheap grace" here in getting free of our dependency. Jim learned, in time and with frequent attendance at DA meetings, that the price of freedom from the uneasiness and hollow feelings he felt was every day to trust in the Higher Power and turn his sadness over to this God of his as he understood Him.

Jim mentioned how he had felt an anger toward mem-

bers of the group at his first meetings, for what he felt
was a phoniness in *acting* as though they were feeling
better when in reality he felt that they were putting on a
show. If there is anything a depressed person has a difficult time with it is with someone being cheerful or happy.
When we are feeling bad we think that if we ever did
smile our face would crack. It was when Jim felt he had
no place to go but up, and when his pain got greater than
his own fears of himself needing help, he admitted finally
to the group that his life was unmanageable and out of
control. He also admitted that he had seriously thought
of taking his life as he had just about lost all hope of
removing this sadness which, like a cancer, was taking
his life by inches. It was only when he no longer had
anything to lose that *he made a decision to turn his mind and
his will over to the care of God, as he understood Him*. It was
at this point that the God of his understanding or the
Higher Power was allowed to work in Jim's life. God
doesn't act like a gangbuster and force His way into our
lives – He has to be invited. Once again there is an invitation from us and we admit our dependence on Him
instead of on our own addiction. It is then that our feelings
begin to come alive and the flow of God's love makes its
way into our lives. We begin to find that we are feeling
better and that something good, even though ever so
slightly, is beginning to stir within us. There is a feeling
of newness that comes over us as we trust, possibly for
the first time, this God who will give us our heart's desire.
**"God grant us the serenity to accept the things we cannot
change, the courage to change the things that we can and
the wisdom to know the difference."** Trust God to be
God and let this Power help you, as it has helped millions
of other men and women before you!

At step three, many of us said to our Maker, as we understood him: "God, I offer myself to Thee – to build with me and to do with me as Thou wilt. Relieve me of the bondage of self, that I may better do Thy will. Take away my difficulties, that my transcendence over them may bear witness to those I would help of Thy Power, Thy love, and Thy way of life. May I do Thy will always!" (1).

Sue's Story

Probably my earliest memory is one of depression – I remember getting a spanking from my father (I don't remember what for) at about the age of two or three years. He kept on whipping me because I was crying and snivelling. I thought he would kill me because I kept on snivelling and couldn't stop. He said he would keep it up until I did stop. I quickly learned that crying was a "no-no", and any other expression of emotion was a "no-no".

In my family people did not cry, laugh, smile or show any emotions, above all not LOVE. We were also superior to other people, were more intelligent, were more wealthy, achieved more and in general, were never "common". Did we ever carry the British "stiff upper lip" to new heights! Many people comment on my mother's beautiful face. She is eighty years old now and still has practically no wrinkles. I know her beauty secret – it is staying inside out of the sun (never sweat or go places outside, where there just might be "common" people) and never show any emotion!

I only saw my father kiss my mother once, a brief, cold peck on the cheek as she was being wheeled off to surgery. I was an only child for twelve years, after six years of marriage (no wonder!). My father was an alcoholic, my mother possibly one (at least in my teens and until my father's death). My father had wanted to be a doctor and was very disappointed that I was a girl, and made no secret of it. He must have decided he would have to "make do", and as early as I can remember I was told that I would be a doctor. In my childhood at Christmas, I always got a doctor's kit and never one for nurses.

My family did not do things together such as picnics or going to ball games or movies. If I went anywhere it was with a girlfriend's family, or my father drove me and picked me up afterwards. The only thing my family enjoyed was food (no wonder we are all overweight).

In school, I made good grades in kindergarten. I got a "U" (unsatisfactory) for conduct (talking too much). My father told me that if I got another I would get beaten with his razor strap. When I got another "U" in conduct, I started crying and the teacher asked me why. When I told her she erased it and said it was a mistake. When my father saw the report card, he thought *I* had erased it and I was whipped anyway! I quickly learned that I had a job, that of earning good grades so that I could get into medical school. It was hard for a woman to get into medical school then.

At the age of sixteen, I fell in love for the first time. He was a few years older (he had been in the Navy), and he was clever enough to sit and listen to my father talk for hours about hunting and fishing. We broke up because he insisted on running away to get married. I knew I had to finish High School. I was so depressed then that I really wanted to die.

I met my husband-to-be when I was a senior in High School. We met in church at the Christmas Eve candlelight service. He was handsome and very polite and well mannered. After a while, we became sexually active. This was both because of my being starved of love and the image I had of my father's fury if he ever found out!

In my senior year at High School, I decided I wanted to be an engineer and design household appliances with features and conveniences that women would appreciate. I visited the Dean of the local University and talked with him and he was enthusiastic. I came home excited and proud but imagine the angry fit my father had when I told him. He told me that he would not pay one penny of the tuition and that I would have to earn my living and my tuition unless I went to medical school.

I became more defiant after I entered college (premed). I got married at the age of eighteen, quit college and moved to Florida with my husband Fred. We weren't able to earn a living in Florida so we came back to Louisville. After we were married a year or so, and after my first daughter was born, I noticed that Fred was drinking heavily on weekends and then it progressed to every night. At least he went out to drink and didn't do it at home like my father. When I was pregnant with my second daughter, I found out that Fred was having an affair. I became very depressed then and we separated. All during my marriage, my family pushed me to divorce him. I forgave him, but he continued drinking and was never at home, until finally after ten years of marriage he got a young girl pregnant and I realized that he was not a real father to the children anyway, so I divorced him and went back to live with my parents.

I had worked for a doctor, who was much older than me and who was highly respected in the community and in his church (he was a Deacon). He was a real father figure to me. He paid my college tuition for me to attend night classes. I was studying to be a Certified Medical Assistant. I completed the college courses shortly after the time of my divorce. While going to college I was working and dating someone I really cared about, but he was transferred out of town. The doctor I worked for was giving me amphetamines so I could sometimes go for days without sleeping. I was really taking them a lot to keep going, then he gave me sleeping pills to sleep. I didn't realize what this was doing to me. When I got my divorce, the doctor made some strong sexual advances to me and I quit my job. I had to go to Lawrence, Kansas to take the Certification Test. I was so depressed about the divorce, the doctor's advances when I had trusted him, my loss of the boyfriend and my job, and I thought I had failed the Test (I hadn't, I was the first person in Kentucky to pass), that I deliberately overdosed on sleeping pills and alcohol in my motel room in Kansas. The man in the next room heard me when I collapsed and the management called an ambulance and I recovered.

My family was so severe with me when I lived with them that I tried again. This time I was working for another doctor and had read the "perfect" way to overdose in his medical journal. Unfortunately my mother heard me when I fell down the stairs and I awoke in a psychiatric ward. At least the psychiatrist knew that I loved animals and he told me that my taking amphetamines was like beating a dying horse, so I quit taking them and would never take them again. Unfortunately, I had shock treatments which didn't help my depression and filled me with extreme fear of further treatment. I came out of the hospital to face all my old problems of trying to rear two children with only what I could earn, no family support or love and no real help. The doctor I worked for this time had fired me and I had a hard time finding another job. I finally got one as a Medical Transcriber at a hospital. I liked this better because there was less contact with people and I could never trust working for a doctor again.

I continued this occupation for about twenty-five years. I had bouts of severe depression and was always at least somewhat depressed and mostly a recluse after my children were grown. But I thought this was all there was to life and I really had no hope of anything different. I had tried some anti-depressants but had such severe side effects I could not take them.

As if this was not enough, in May 1989, I came down with a virus that caused brachial plexopathy and could not hold my arms up to type, so I was disabled. I found that it would take months before I could begin getting disability payments. I quickly went through my meagre savings and was in terror of becoming homeless, since my family would not help me.

I had started counselling with Hugh Smith, but my dear, dear family thought I needed medicine (and probably hospitalization). At their insistence, I went to a local free clinic. The psychiatrist put me on [a certain drug] and after three days, I felt myself becoming really aggressive (I could have hit just about anyone) but I realized it and quit. I definitely feel this drug should be taken off the market. The psychiatrist at the clinic then put me on another drug, which made me want to sleep all the time. At the group sessions, I immediately saw that the members all looked and acted like zombies. They told me to keep coming and I would get better like they were! For activities they strung beads and made muffins! One good look at them and depression (or even suicide) did not look so bad.

About this time Hugh Smith started DA and I went to a meeting. I learned that the other members had the same problems, some had attempted suicide, but they were getting better and without being drugged into a stupor. I had always believed in Christ, even though my family did not attend church. I really thank my Higher Power for leading me to the church where Hugh Smith is a counsellor. Here the priest says that God loves us just as we are (not if we will change or be something else). The congregation is a very loving, supporting one and so this made following the twelve steps easier for me. It was no trouble for me to realize that I was powerless over depression and that my life was unmanageable (Step 1). By looking at the faces and talking with the other members, I could see that they had obtained peace (Step 2). From there, Step 3, turning my will and life over to the care of God, as I understand Him, was easy. I just pictured myself struggling in the water, but if you stop struggling in the water and just give up and lie on your back, you will float!

Action does precede motivation and I began working at our local zoo. It is a beautiful place (and safe from muggers too). I began talking with people and learned about classes there to become a docent (volunteer teacher). I enrolled and graduated, which gives me a new purpose in life. I get great joy from working there doing outreaches to schools, nursing homes and hospitals, and have made friends, both animals and humans. There isn't a day that I go there to talk that I don't get thanked by someone, a visitor or employee (or sometimes an animal).

My family, they haven't changed (although my mother commented on the change in my face) but I have! In this, the Serenity Prayer really helps. I know that I can't change them, but I have new friends and a real support system so this doesn't matter so much now.

Whoever you are, you who are reading this, BELIEVE! The first three steps are the most important. Walking or other exercise is important. Staying with it is important. Going to the meetings and participating is important but above all else, FAITH is important – it will truly move mountains!

Step Four

Made a Searching and Fearless Moral Inventory of Ourselves

Tom asked why we needed step four in our recovery. He said that he was depressed and didn't need anything else to make him feel worse – like dredging up things that he might have done in the past. Why, Tom wondered, should he resurrect old ghosts? Anyway, when he spoke about a moral inventory it reminded him of religion with its do's and don'ts with special emphasis on the don'ts. Tom said he came into DA to learn about what was making him depressed and that he didn't need anything else to make him feel guilty or sadder.

Some people think that for a person to dredge up old hurts and wrongs will make them that much more depressed. I guess it depends on what types of stuff we put on our inventory. The following list of defects of character can help our sadness persist: for example, our perfectionism, our need to control, our fears, guilt, shame or resentments, dishonesty, selfishness, passivity, anger, indecisiveness, fear of change or finally the inability to live with uncertainty. When we begin to ask God for help in removing these areas from our life, this asking for help will not make us more depressed – it will in fact make us more hopeful. In step three we said we make a decision. This means just that and not just a promise as it says in the *AA Big Book*. When we begin to surrender our will and our life to the Higher Power and are willing to *expose* our defects to others in the group it is then that our life may be able to take on a peace coupled with new purpose.

This really is an essential and necessary step that has to be taken if we want to leave our prison of depression behind. We must not only make a searching inventory of how we view ourselves, our world and our future, but we must also take stock of any character defects that keep us locked into personal feelings of shame and guilt. We need to look at the areas that Dorothy Rowe has identified in her book *Depression: The Way Out Of Your Prison* (17) where she lists the six major beliefs of persons who get themselves depressed. All depressed people hold all these beliefs in one degree or another. She contends that most depressed people hold these facts about themselves as immutable truths, unchanging and set in granite. They think nothing will ever change in their lives. These beliefs become the sort of material that we need to list if we are to get free of the depression that has played such a big role in our lives.

The first immutable belief, according to Dorothy Rowe, that many depressed hold onto, like the inspired words from God, is the belief that no matter how good and nice I appear to be, I am really bad, evil, valueless, unacceptable to myself and to others.

Step four is a critical step if we want to begin the journey toward wholeness, peace and having good feelings about ourselves again. But if we want to stay in the pit of sadness then the belief that we are worthless and not quite good enough will definitely limit our awareness of what we can become and what we can do for ourselves. I believe a lot of our difficulties have their roots in our need to be perfect and to do things the way others expect. It's as though we have to take care of their needs before our own. Significant persons from our past have promoted the belief that for me to be acceptable I had to do things their way and their way alone. I had to please them or I might be abandoned and left alone forever. This in itself is a frightening situation for any of us. I needed continually to attempt to be someone other than myself. I constantly was filled with a sadness, as I never felt I could measure up to what others wanted me to do or be. My whole life was graded on what others thought I should be. Good was never good enough and so I continued to test the limits in an effort to excel but the limits were never clearly marked out. I sensed that somehow I couldn't ever measure up to others' expectations and that made me feel ashamed of myself. Not only did I feel guilt but I also felt ashamed – ashamed that my inadequacies would be exposed for everyone to see and ridicule. My constant fear was that others would see how bad I really was.

This is how the inventory can help us unearth and eradicate those character defects as we begin to see the truth manifest itself and as we take stock of our lives. We need to learn how to give ourselves the good breaks that we would give any other human being instead of our self-bashing. Any compliment given to us we immediately deny and act as if it doesn't really apply – especially, we think, if people knew the real me. We continually perpetuate the belief that we are no good and worthless, because of past childhood beliefs still unconsciously influencing our present thoughts and behaviour. These past events, some not even consciously remembered, are somehow still driving the sadness in our daily lives. This vague feeling of being a mistake and feeling that we are just tolerated by others is a belief that must be dismantled and thrown on the junk heap if we are to be the happy persons that we are meant to be. We are mourning part of ourselves that was never able to be given expression and this makes us sad. When we bring up this fact at our meetings we hear how others in the group likewise had no childhood and that the ability to have fun was terribly missing in our youngest years. Spontaneity and a childlike frivolity were considered out of place in many of our homes. Children were not allowed to talk about their feelings or even to trust them. All of this put us at risk for depression as we swallowed feelings that we weren't allowed to express.

We need to get down on paper our feelings about ourselves and locate where we got our first impressions of ourselves. What type of attitudes did we grow up with in our homes regarding our parents and siblings? Were there family secrets that weren't allowed to be talked about outside our home? Did we ever see our parents showing affection for one another? Did we frequently observe our parents fighting? Did we fear as youngsters that Mum and Dad might abandon us and that we might end up being orphans? If our parents did divorce did we blame ourselves for their divorce? It is precisely in doing the inventory that we can bring out our feelings of shame and early feelings of embarrassment because of how these significant persons from childhood made us feel about ourselves.

I still remember feeling embarrassed when my third grade teacher told me in front of the whole class that I would never be like my brother who was much smarter than I. I used to feel my face get hot every time I thought about that embarrassing incident. But the more I share my shame of having been exposed to others about something that I had no control over, the more free I become of that fear. The same principle is at work here in the DA group. We can take our own personal inventory of our weaknesses and fears and trust the group to hear us out and accept our stories of shame and hurt as we accept theirs. We begin to see how and why so many people feel bad because in their earlier years people made them feel that they could never measure up to the way others expected them to grow up. By becoming our little child once more, we paradoxically grow up.

We have made the decision to turn our wills and our lives over to the care of God as we understand Him and this in itself will help us to get honest within ourselves and with the members of the group. This honesty will set us free as we pull ourselves away from the old self that we once were and begin to be in touch with our deepest and truest selves. Our exhaustive and honest search into ourselves will begin to reveal to us that so much of what we thought to be evil or worthless in our earlier lives was a scaffold built on sand. Character is built by truth and the willingness to list the truths in ourselves. It can be a painful search but it will reveal that it's all right to be imperfect and not to have all the answers and not to be perfect. It's all right to trust others with our deepest fears and hurts, and to know that we can still be loved and respected even though we share how bad and evil we have considered ourselves over the years. It will be evident in time that one's feeling of deep sadness did not come out of nowhere but indeed was the result of the way we were led to believe and think about ourselves.

"To thine own self be true" is an old axiom that has much merit for those of us who work the spiritual programme of the twelve steps. Often in therapy I ask people to list as many strengths as they can, and for some this is a difficult task when they are depressed and the world appears to be a grey and fearsome dark place. But this is the inventory that we must make – we must begin to look at our strengths and stop wallowing in the self-pity which denies the new directions and progress occurring in our lives through the love of the Higher Power in our individual lives. This is the major character defect of our depression, namely that we can't seem to see the gracious goodness in ourselves that has been placed there from all time by the Higher Power. This in itself is the attitude that keeps alive our depression, sadness and self-deprecating attitudes. We need to look at our assets and list our strengths as we gather together time after time in our DA group or in our individual working of the twelve-step programme in our lives. We likewise need to remove as quickly as possible all the old excuses and reasons that we cling to and that keep us depressed and out of healthful recovery. Let's be objective about ourselves and admit that just as we have caused ourselves to be depressed we likewise can undepress ourselves in the same way.

We are not here to condemn ourselves but to evaluate how we can achieve an inner peace and serenity that is promised to those who let go of their sadness and proceed to trust in their Higher Power or God as they understand Him. It won't do all that good to try to search out the *why* of our depressions but what must be discovered is the *how* to begin to reverse this sad state of affairs in our lives now. Our family and teachers and our unhappy experiences taught us to believe that we were bad and valueless, but we are free to change that belief. We must realize that we are responsible for the way we feel and that we can't blame it on our childhood, parents, significant others or the weather. We must take responsibility for the way we behave. It is without doubt that the more we begin to talk to ourselves in a positive and regular way the more we are able to develop the habit of acting in a consistantly positive life-giving way. First of all we must motivate ourselves to some type of action if we are to emerge successfully from our continued state of sadness and lethargy.

The second immutable truth, according to Dorothy Rowe, is that "Other people are such that I must fear, hate and envy them." If we believe that we are bad and valueless then it follows that we must fear other people because they can find out how bad we are and reject us. When we fear anyone for long enough we come to hate that person, and when we fear someone we don't get close enough to that person to see his difficulties, we think he is having an easy time, and so we envy him. So you will believe that everyone around you is an enemy. It's most difficult to learn to live in trust if you are in a constant state of terror of those around you. We need to look at all our relationships and seek out the people for whom we presently have these strong feelings of hate, envy and fear. We have to root out of ourselves all those strong emotions which are like bars of steel keeping us locked up in these emotions of powerlessness. It is only when we are able to look honestly into our souls that we will begin to see that it is how we feel about others that has a present influence on our feelings today. Sometimes envious and fearful thoughts bring up some very sad feelings, and whenever we need to feel back in control we immediately drop back into a sad feeling – it keeps us from having to feel too much. We are much like the practising alcoholic taking one more drink to medicate and numb unpleasant feelings.

Sadness is likewise an addiction in that it is used to blunt a very painful loss, a thought of a future loss or to numb the way our world happens to be experienced by us today. We would do well to track the times that we become sad as well as track the automatic thoughts that continually throw us into a state of despair. It's very much like the nicotine addiction where the smoking addict who is trying to stop smoking keeps track of where, when and how many cigarettes he/she smokes a day. He or she keeps an inventory of the difference it makes when with certain people or when engaged in different activities. Do some people, places or things cause him/her to smoke more or less? All this can help list the problem areas, the areas that are filled with stress which causes him/her to experience some relief from the pain. So, we need to look more closely at the times we sink ourselves back into the pit of depression.

We also might find that our self-confidence has greatly diminished since we have been depressed and so we need to realize that if we are able to regain any skills in relating to others then we must get out of our little circle of life and get involved with others like ourselves in a DA group. We also need to realize that this step four is only for ourselves: it would be comfortable to sit back and blame others for the way our lives have turned out – but we can make the inventory only of ourselves, take responsibility for ourselves and admit that we are the cause of how we feel. It's at this point that we claim responsibility for self and can honestly say that our inventory is a searching and fearless one.

Denial, projection and rationalization are major defence mechanisms of those persons who are sadding them-

selves. Over the years they have denied that their
behaviour is abnormal or that they have any control over
the way they feel. Also, people who are addicted to sadness in their lives may have projected onto someone else
the blame for the way they have felt all these past years.
They also tend to rationalize that since someone hurt them
in the past they have the right to sad themselves today.

When we interact with people who have tried to understand themselves and their need for such defences we can
come to understand the way we use these defences and
then give up our dependence on them.

Being socially isolated is a key component in most people's depression. The fact that many depressed people
prefer to sit and stew in their isolation and pain precludes
their feeling better. It is only when we can get past the
blaming of others, the denying of our own ability to
choose a healthier way to live and think that our
depression will wither away for lack of attention. But
making the decision to turn our wills and our lives over
to the care of God as we understand Him is the beginning
of the end for our depressing lifestyle. The self-help group
of *Depressed Anonymous* makes it possible, if you choose,
to find men and women to whom you need not apologize
for your depression. You will not be judged for it.

A clear light seems to fall upon us all – when we open
our eyes. Since our blindness is caused by our own
defects, we must first deeply realize what they are.
Constructive meditation is the first requirement for each
new step in our spiritual growth. (4)

Step Five

Admitted to God,
to Ourselves and to Another
Human Being the Exact Nature
of our Wrongs

Mary couldn't understand how this step five had anything to do with her. She hadn't done anything wrong to anybody. She was coming to DA to find a way out of the sadness which always seemed to play a large part of her life.

She did know that her parents were practising alcoholics, and she lived in constant terror as a child because of their constant bickering and fighting when they were drunk. Because of shame, Mary was never able to share her story with any of her friends. In time she began to think that her feelings were disloyal to her parents, whom she felt she had to love because they were her parents. She said she got confused because they seemed to want her around sometimes but at other times they told her what a worthless and lazy girl she was. The thing that hurt most, she said, is that she believed them. So, now she wonders how this fifth step applies to her when it's her parents who need to admit their wrongs to her. Mary was puzzled. All she wants to do is to get over some of the anger that she still holds for the way her parents neglected her when she was growing up. She says that every time she goes back home a sadness seems just to come over her – as though out of the blue – and for no apparent reason. She also says that her stomach gets all knotted up.

Everyone who works the programme, like Mary, is very much aware that if they want peace and serenity then they have to continue this search into themselves. The only condition for those who want to join the DA group is a sincere desire to stop sadding themselves. And as Mary learned from the other members of DA, it wasn't until she could let out her feelings of anger and rage – a little at a time – that she began to feel better.

The fifth step is usually done with another member of the DA group or any other person who is working the twelve-step programme in their own life. When you want to start cleaning house and stop blaming others for the way you feel, and take responsibility for yourself, then you know that you are in earnest about beginning your programme.

There is a saying that "When a ship is in a storm and in danger, dump the cargo, and save the ship". You have been brought to a point in your life, be it a young life or an older life, where you can begin to dump some of the garbage of your past. It is in working the twelve steps – inch by inch getting better. The freedom that you feel is marvellous as you begin to see that there is a light at the end of the tunnel. There is hope and it feels good.

In *Depression: The Way Out Of Your Prison*, Dorothy

Rowe lists the third immutable belief as "Life is terrible and death is worse". Many depressed persons find themselves in this bind. You are on the horns of a dilemma – you feel that you can't ever win and you see no way out of this everlasting sadness, and so you get used to your sad thoughts and continue to isolate yourself from the real world and others. If you want to free yourself from the horns of this dilemma you have to ask yourself as well as members of the group what it is that makes you feel that life is so terrible and sad.

So many times it is our *perfectionism* that makes life so difficult and we never seem able to meet the challenge of our own unrealistic goals and ambitions. We never can do it quite well enough. We need to be able to trust that we can make mistakes. In my past, it has not been permissible to do that. It is this continual search for ways to be perfect that drives us back to sadness and the misery of our addiction. We believe that we will never have a respite from the pain of our loneliness, and that the hell of our existence can only be relieved by numbing our sensitive feelings. We do this by withdrawing contact from others. We often need to admit to God and others that we love to play the martyr role and have others tell us what a "saint" we are for all the awful things that we have had to put up with for so many years. This is what we want to hear. At least someone knows the hell we've been through. As a martyr we are waiting to be rewarded for our goodness. Once we give up this idea we know not only in our head but also in our heart, that this totally accepting Higher Power to which we surrender is always ready to accept us as we are – not as we think we should be.

For many of us it's our own sense of worthlessness that we need to look at and admit to God, another human

being and ourselves, that this self-pity and low self-esteem
are not what God wants us to experience. It is relatively
easy to tell God some of the garbage that is part of the
burden that we carry around but the big job is to admit
to another person our failings, faults and weaknesses.
Really to get something out of step five you must share
your pain with another person. It is in the sharing of our
sins and wrongs that gradually we are freed from the
shame, guilt and fear that keep us in the prison of our
depression.

How many excuses we can think up to prevent us from
going to friends to tell them the exact nature of our wrong.
We can think of so many reasons why we can't tell others
why we are the way we are. For many of us who need
to be perfect we have a difficult time telling someone else
that we might not be what we appear to be.

We must see ourselves as we really are. If we are ever
sad about people we have hurt, or even more so angry
about people who have hurt us over the years, then we
need to get this out in the open. We also need to share
the anger inside us that has been swallowed for so many
years and which likewise needs to be expressed. We need
to get in touch with the feelings of rage that have been
under our tight control over the years. So many times we
have felt that if we ever let go of our rage it would fling
us completely out of control and we would experience
complete annihilation. What we need to discover is that
whatever emotion we express – anger, tears, laughter –
does not go on forever but comes naturally to an end.

The fourth immutable belief that the depressed person
has is that since bad things happened in the past only
bad things will happen in the future. This belief that rules
so many of our lives seems such an accurate fact: we can't
ever trust the fact that we might feel good again. In fact,

our misery is such a predictable part of our lives that we are afraid to step out and think differently or live with any amount of hope, because this new happy feeling won't last anyway. How many times have I heard people who have been depressed for as many years as they can remember not want to give up and let go of the feeling that makes them miserable. They would rather stay mired down in the pain of their sadness than risk a chance in the sunlight of hope and serenity. I can understand how people would be afraid of trusting God to let them feel hope and peace because all they have known is the pain of their depression – but at the same time I believed others in the group who tell us how they took the risk to turn their minds and wills over to the care of God, and how their trust, as small as a mustard seed, began to bring them out of their sadness and despair. You have to be brutally honest with yourself and really want to escape from depression. You do this by admitting your own need to be depressed and your own fear of the alternative, namely taking charge of your life and assuming full responsibility for the way you think, feel and behave. It's much safer to remain depressed.

Many times we hear how depression is anger turned inward. This is one way to explain it. Depression is also a way to keep from assuming our rightful place in the world and society. You must tell others that your very fear of the future and of others is the very thing that builds your prison. You need to surrender the fears and hurts of your life. You need to give them up to the Higher Power or to God as you understand Him. It is with this in mind that you begin to gain more insights and honesty in your life. Others in the DA group will also help you see that you can blame the other people in your life for your problems all you want, but it is only when you no longer see yourself as *victim* that you can stand up and say that you no longer choose to stay depressed. "I am going to enjoy life and hope for good things to begin to happen to me", you can say. I think sometimes we must confess that we liked being called a "depressive" as it made us feel as though we couldn't help being the way we were and, of course, we know this isn't true. Once we admit our victim stance and no longer consider ourselves as permanent sufferers of depression, then this honesty can release a new sense of identity for ourselves. The support of the group will also allow me to say that I don't have to be what I was any more. I don't need it!

The fifth immutable belief that builds hopelessness in us is the belief that it is wrong to get angry. We have learned from childhood that not only do little girls not show anger, but little boys likewise were made to believe that any type of outward expression of one's unpleasant feelings was not permissible. We believed that we had no right to be angry. To be always smiling and happy means you are good; to experience and express the emotion of anger is a sign that you are out of control, and being out of control is bad. But if anything can cause us to be depressed it is a lifetime of swallowing our anger. This might have its roots in our childhood when we were abused, physically, emotionally or even sexually, by a parent, relative or guardian. The mere thought of this might throw us into a deep sense of personal worthlessness and rage until we are able to get in touch with it. Sometimes this rage is so powerful that we have to numb ourselves so as not to feel the power of it and so be afraid that it will destroy our very selves.

We don't advocate that you come to DA meetings and take your anger out on anybody there, but we do advocate that persons begin to allow themselves to feel this anger inside them and when they do they will soon talk about some of these feelings that might for some go back a long time. Again, it is my experience that the people who come and stay with DA are those who have been depressing most of their lives. Now, by their active participation in the programme, they have discovered a group of men and women who speak the same language and who are helping others learn how to leave their depression if they so choose. But when we are angry we need to say that we are angry about this or that person, this or that experience, and then feel it – don't run from it or act as though it's not there, but get in touch with the feeling and see what it's saying to you, now. You won't die from feeling it; you will be more by feeling it.

Some people have found that just saying to another person that they have done something they are ashamed of can in itself help them find a new acceptance of themselves that they have never felt before. A good fifth step covers all the major areas of our lives that we need to look at and for which we ask God's forgiveness. A good way to start is to be willing to make a list of all the major wrongs in our life and then take these to a trusted friend, and tell him or her the exact nature of our wrongs.

The sixth immutable belief that you must hold to if you want to stay depressed is that you must never forgive anyone, least of all yourself. This is a sure-fire way to make certain you stay depressed. Most persons who stay depressed are experts at this one and know that they are so bad that no one can ever forgive them for all the bad things they have done in the past. Of course, the depressed people realize after a number of DA meetings that they have a tendency to make mountains out of mole-hills and so any little thing that they might have done wrong is ruminated upon time and again until they have taken the role of judge and executioner of their very own selves. They turn their mistakes, sins and inadequacies over and over again in their minds until that is all they can think of. This is the nature of an addiction; the compulsion to repeat becomes the habit.

It is this attitude of unforgiveness that freezes the depressed person's life in the past tense and forces her/him to live in the painful past of pain and pressure of real or imagined sins. The depressed person can't believe that all things are forgiveable.

I think that many depressed people need to admit that they are harder on themselves than anyone else would be. I'm sure that if they heard someone else tell of a situation the same as theirs, the depressed person would be the first one to show and extend them forgiveness and compassion. Depression feeds on hurt, pain and self-doubt. When we are depressed we have a need to bash ourselves for our imagined crimes and sinfulness. The fifth step, if done genuinely and prayerfully, will in time help restore our sense of freedom and belief that we are truly forgiven. It is the miracle of the group and its acceptance, love and nurture that helps the depressed person feel secure without recourse to depression.

Many times persons who come to DA come because of a broken marriage, loss of love, of a job, or of one's self-esteem. People tell members of the group that they have never respected themselves, their own intuitions or anything else that was good in themselves. If they stay with the programme they will have to admit that they have ignored their good points and remained afraid and penned up in the isolation of their feelings of worthlessness. This is where the depressed need to start their checklist and admit that they have seen themselves as bad and unacceptable; that they have envied and feared others; that they thought life was terrible and death was worse; that only bad things could happen to them in the future because only bad things had happened to them in the past; that they didn't allow themselves to express emotions; and that they never forgave themselves or anyone else. One's personal recovery begins by telling God as we understand Him that we surrender all these defects of character, and that because of them our lives have been unmanageable. Our recovery begins the minute we make the decision to turn our minds and our wills over to the care of God as we understand Him.

By our continual shutting ourselves up in the little world of our own mind we gradually sink more and more into despair, and feel that no one can understand how we think and feel. The biggest freedom that we can gain from confessing to someone else is that we no longer have to have it all together and be perfect. We can begin to admit it when we are petty, selfish and self-centred. We can then admit that we want to have restored a sense of peace by getting free from all worry and fear from the past and by turning these over to the Higher Power. We can then discover that forgiving ourselves and being forgiven by God are one and the same thing. The group will see to it that the more you admit your own fears about yourself and the future, the less terror the present will hold for you.

Alcoholics Anonymous have found that

When we decide who is to hear our story, we waste no time. We have a written inventory and we are prepared for a long talk. We explain to our partner what we are about to do and why we have to do it.

We pocket our pride and go to it, illuminating every twist of character, every dark cranny of the past. Once we have taken this step, withholding nothing, we are delighted. We can look the world in the eye. We can be alone at perfect peace and ease. Our fears fall from us. We begin to feel the nearness of our Creator. We may have had certain spiritual beliefs, but now we begin to have a spiritual experience . . . (1)

My dear friends, it is this spiritual experience, to feel God is with you, and that this is the joy that will restore your youth and renew your spirit. We no longer have to be the way we are; we can choose to feel and be different. Others are doing it; so can you!

Robin's Story

Part of the *Depressed Anonymous*'s preamble states that "you are about to experience the magic of the [DA] group. You are to begin a journey of hope." This is perhaps the best way for me to describe my personal experience with *Depressed Anonymous*. Through this twelve-step programme, I have been on a journey of transformation from the familiar life of drudgery, gloom and desperation to discovering a new freedom and a new happiness – something I didn't know existed.

Prior to my intervention with the group, I felt as though I didn't fit in and I was on a desperate search for happiness. Over the years I had tried so many remedies: isolation, very monogamous relationships, long rides alone in the mountains (on my horse), reading "How to be Happy" books, pursuing a bachelor's degree, staying busy and even moving nine hundred miles away from my family and friends (talk about a geographical cure!). Through the group, I have come to recognize that deep inside I was miserable, suffering from low self-esteem and yearning to be loved and to be accepted "as an equal".

Since my childhood, unconditional love was a word I truly did not comprehend. In order to gain my parents' affection, I had to please people. Today I am grasping the meaning of unconditional love through the fellowship of

DA. Now it's OK to be me. There are no "conditions" being placed on me. It doesn't matter if I make mistakes or say the wrong things. No one in this DA group will jeer me. Here is truly a place where I can say whatever is on my mind and still be capable of receiving love and acceptance.

My entire perspective is changing. Other people whom I once thought were judgemental are now considered as all being a child of God – all created equal. What a peace provocative tool this is! Really! It helps lift those negative attitudes and replaces them with affirmations. This is certainly the most valuable technique offered in *Depressed Anonymous*: to acquire an optimistic attitude towards life itself, or simply "making gratitude my attitude". So many of us were only familiar with the sham and drudgery of life, but even with all the sham and drudgery in the world, it is still a beautiful place to live. We learn to change *not* the world, but how we view the world and all its intricacies.

Using the twelve steps allows me to begin that journey of hope and to admit that I am powerless over depression. There are times when depression overwhelms me so intensely that it nearly cripples me altogether. Those emotions of failure, shame and "feeling less" than, become so uncontrollable that I have to stop and simply admit that I am powerless over them. But now I truly believe that there is a power greater than myself and greater than those emotions. This Higher Power (whom I choose to call God) is there to help me any time I ask Him. And you know what? He rescues me every single time!

Step Six

We're entirely ready
to have God remove all our
Shortcomings

There is a list of seven character defects that have been traditionally called the seven deadly sins. Even though the total list is not familiar to many of us, most have been experienced by all of us at one time or another in our life. The seven deadly sins are pride, laziness, gluttony, envy/jealousy, greed, lust and dishonesty.

When we realize that we are going to let God as we understand Him remove the defects of our character it is clear that we have to let go and let God do His work in our lives. We are saying that we are going to allow God to remove those defects of character that keep pulling us back into the experience of depression. We know that our depression is what keeps us from other people, as well as keeping our feelings frozen and out of touch with our real selves. The first five steps have brought us to this point where we now admit to someone else and to God the exact nature of our wrongs. We have made a confession and come right. We revealed our secrets to some other human being and this released in us a freedom never before felt, until we were ready to have God remove our defects. By our admission that we aren't perfect and that our lives have been out of control we can begin to get our problems out into the light of day. By trusting others with our deepest hurts and fears this sometimes can reduce the size of these very same obstacles to happiness. We might also have felt God's presence for the first time as we began to experience a new sense of peace living inside of us.

When we look back, we realize that the things which came to us when we put ourselves in God's hands were better than anything we could have planned. (1)

It is now that we need the strength of humility to face ourselves and declare that we are a broken and hurting individual, and that our addiction to depression has kept us from really living and trusting in God/Higher Power. Once we have dug out in steps four and five what has been the cause of our chronic descent into hopelessness, we can not only seek out the solution to our patterns of dysfunction but can now list our strengths. We need to begin to identify our positive strengths and depend on them if we are to move towards hope and a sense of mastery over our lives. Many people, for a lot of reasons, are blind to the fact that they are addicted to depression, and continue to live in a state of denial and rationalization about their need to sad themselves. They are *sadd*icts.

*Sadd*icts believe that it is much better to choose to live in a state of misery than to choose to live in a state of serenity by letting God remove their defects of character. So many people choose the predictableness of misery to the risky feeling of being unsure and scared over the new and faint feelings of lightness and cheer. As the depressed person gradually begins to knock down the wall of his or her denial that he or she is addicted to sadness whenever life gets stressful, this in itself is the starting point in the recovery process. Most of us tend to avoid the unfamiliar and stay with what we know. We are like the practising alcoholic who, whenever he/she meets a stressful or unpleasant person, place or memory, starts to medicate themselves with alcohol. The overeater, gambler, smoker, sexual addict are all driven by their compulsions. The emptiness of our lives is like a hole that continually needs to be filled with some compulsive and addictive behaviour. By letting go of our excessive tightfisted hold on our life, which paradoxically itself causes us to lose hold, we start to face reality for the first time without the crippling crutch of our compulsion. We let go of our compulsion to repeat – the ritual of addictions.

My depression deepened unbearably, and finally it seemed to me as though I were at the very bottom of the pit. For the moment, the last vestige of my proud obstinacy was crushed. All at once I found myself crying out, "If there is a God, let Him show Himself! I am ready to do anything, anything!"

Suddenly the room lit up with a great white light. It seemed to me, in the mind's eye, that I was on a mountain and that a wind not of air but of spirit was blowing. And then it burst upon me that I was a free man. Slowly the ecstasy subsided. I lay on the bed, but now for a time I was in another world, a new world of consciousness. All about me and through me there was a wonderful feeling of Presence, and I thought to myself, "So this is the God of the preachers!" (1)

It takes getting to a point where all we can do is surrender and let go of our own will and let God be in charge of our lives. In the case of Bill W., one of the founders of Alcoholics Anonymous, he pleaded to God for help and admitted that he was ready to do anything, anything to get relief. This uncovering of what God wants for us will help us see how we need to change the way we act, feel and think. I have heard many say that they would love to get rid of their depression, meaning they would no longer depress themselves if they could be sure that there wouldn't be any more pain. Of course, you and I know that this can't be possible. Bill W. stated that pain is the touchstone of spiritual progress.

A character defect is something that we all suffer from and it is in working the twelve-step programme that we discover how to overcome these defects. Normally as an addictive personality, as we have mentioned before, we have a hole deep inside of us that we try to fill with food, alcohol, gambling, sex, love, depression, etc. Paradoxically, the continued feeding of our compulsion makes the hole that much deeper. The more we want to experience the temporary comfort of the addiction the more that experience dictates the course of our life's focus. Our whole attention is directed towards getting more of the comforting experience. I am sure that not too many people would think that their lifelong experience with depression was an addiction but I am telling you that it is just that.

I see it as a character defect to continue to choose the chronic state of depression when you could feel hopeful like others who are working the twelve steps and who are trusting the Higher Power to take away their fears, obsessions, and anxieties that they hold for themselves.

According to the medieval Church, pride was the deadliest of the seven deadly sins because *it stopped people from changing*. It is my pride which keeps me from admitting that I am the reason for my own depression. We need the humility to say to God and the group that my life is definitely unmanageable and that it is only the belief in God or the Higher Power that can enable me to move out of this depression.

In this step, as in the fourth and fifth steps, we continue to write out and describe the different character defects that we feel might have got us into trouble along life's way. We began to drop out of life and began to sit back and watch the world go by. We became aware that we weren't having fun any more – if we ever did – and we began to ruminate on how awful we are and how everyone must think we are the worst person ever. Again we need to look at how we see ourselves and admit that we aren't perfect and that that's OK. It's the need to be perfect that keeps us anxious, fearful and helpless. We will realize that we can just be us and that we don't have to live up to anyone else's expectations beside our own.

That we are entirely ready to have God remove our defects of character says that we are no longer going to resist making changes in our life and that we want God to start the work of making us His new creation. This work of having our defects removed takes time – and for most people, a lifetime. The idea is at least to get started and realize that the more you become conscious of areas in your life that need to be looked at, the Higher Power will help you see where you need to put your attention. Very deep, sometimes quite forgotten, damaging emotional conflicts persist below the level of consciousness. At the time of these occurrences, they may have given our emotions violent twists which have since discoloured our personalities and altered our lives for the worse.(3) This is why it is so important to talk with others in your own family about your origins and about those significant people who cared for you when you were a child.

To have lost a parent early in life, either through death or divorce, can have a serious effect on the life of a young child. Early losses in life cause a lot of hurt later on in life and many people think that their depression just happens, out of the blue without rhyme or reason, but usually there IS a reason and most probably it is buried deep in the unconscious because it has been too painful to look at. It is in sharing with a trusted friend, group member(s) or therapist that you can gradually let out the bits of the secret that has been under lock for years. It is also when we can be in contact with persons we trust that the hurts of the past can be revealed.

Now that you have admitted that depression has left you feeling helpless and in its grip you can begin to see how guilt, a sense of shame and losses throughout earlier life might have predisposed one to a depression that now has become a way of life, with the comfort and excuse for not living life to the full!

I think this might be a major stumbling block for many people who come to DA when they hear that they have character defects. For instance, what does all this have to do with their depression? For many people there might be a tendency not to talk about how they hurt, and how they can't allow themselves to grieve life's losses, such as persons whom they love and have lost, a lost job or a childhood that they have never had. For some, retirement can have a crippling effect. Many people are depressed, feel helpless and have no one who understands their situation. At present, in the depth of their depression, they can't begin to think that they might have caused their depression themselves, because the onslaught has been slow and imperceptible. They feel they are going crazy and losing their minds. They feel they can't get another thought into their brain. They also forget easily and can't seem to concentrate much on anything. They also bash themselves unmercifully for all the evil things that they have done. They fear the exposure of their crimes, as they would like to call them, and continue to ruminate on how bad they must be. By pushing down any hopeful or light feelings and preventing them from ever coming to the surface of their mind, they push down all feelings. *When you push down one feeling you push them all down.* We are not dealing with keys on a piano, where one key being depressed has no effect on the one next to it.

It is only when the pain is greater than the fear of talking to someone about their depression that progress begins. The inability to seek help, coupled with how hopeless and dark everything is, makes it quite difficult for the depressed person to come out from his or her darkened world into the light. It is the light of self-love that begins to shine when more revelations are made to someone else about one's sadness and despair and changes begin to occur. When it begins to register in our minds that it is in surrendering that we win, it is then that our lives take on a new turn. We are ready to move forward when we submit to the Higher Power's light operating in our hearts and lives. When we are "entirely ready" means that there will be a full fledged effort on our part to have God assist us in getting through this depression. We have to give this our best. We can't let ourselves be fooled into thinking that we got our depression in the same way that someone would get the flu or catch a cold. We know that somewhere along the path of life we have overloaded the circuits and have felt overwhelmed by a sense of responsibility, guilt or shame, and that this has produced the chronic depression that we can't seem to shake off.

The DA programme based on the twelve steps is a spiritual programme, and one in which you and I continually try to better ourselves and hold off the temptation to depress ourselves when this or that stressful situation, person or memory pushes its way into our minds. It is then that you have to go to the Serenity Prayer and also turn to the Higher Power and tell it that you are not going to depend on a mood of sadness any more but that you are going to depend on it, the Higher Power, to get you through this moment, this hour and this day. You will live one day at a time and stay out of tomorrow, where the anxiety and fear lie, and out of yesterday, where hurt and anger live. This is the only place that we really can be, namely, in today, in this moment, in this hour!

For many of us our fear of others and our need to avoid situations has caused us deep psychic pain and confusion. Any time we feel the need to get off to the quiet and think sad thoughts we become acutely aware that we are not going to do anything hopeful for ourselves. Instead we ask the Higher Power to remove these addictive thoughts and behaviour and grant us the serenity, the will and the courage to look positively to His strength and His power and His will in our personal lives.

Most times when people hear about surrendering their lives to the Higher Power or turning their wills over to God as they understand Him, they find this invitation a most difficult one. So many times people fear that God will have them do something that will cause them pain or that will make their lives unbearable.

As we have said, steps four and five have helped us to uncover our defects and now we are in a position, with the support of the group, to focus in on how certain defects of character have caused us to lose serenity and peace of mind and heart . . . and have caused us to stay imprisoned in our world of sad and negative thoughts and feelings.

In the meetings we hear the positive stories of those members who share with us how their lives were before DA and how their lives are now since they have become active members and are working their programme each day. So many people who were depressed had not taken care of themselves physically or spiritually, and had no close friend with whom to confide their hurts and the storm going on inside themselves. So often it is the person who seems to have lost any meaning for his or her life who is now struggling to find their true self. The recovering members of the DA group continually tell us that they are entirely ready to have their defects of character removed. While accepting God and the group into their lives, their personal letting go has enabled them to experience the presence and peace of God as they understand Him.

> We have emphasized willingness as being indispensable. Are we now ready to let God remove from us all the things which we have admitted are objectionable? Can He take them all – every one? If we still cling to something we will not let go, we ask God to help us to be willing. . . . When ready, we say something like this: "My Creator, I am now willing that you should have all of me, good and bad. I pray that you now remove from me every single defect of character which stands in the way of my usefulness to you and my fellows. Grant me strength, as I go out from here, to do your bidding. Amen!"(1)

We know that our willpower alone can't get us out of this prison of depression, but only a belief in a force or power greater than ourselves. So by working step six we continue to be in God's will and let Him help us discover and root out those defects of character that keep us prisoner.

Lack of power, that was our dilemma. We had to find a power by which we could live, and it had to be a *Power greater than ourselves*(1).

Step Seven

Humbly asked Him to
remove our Shortcomings

We can never really recover from our addictions and find serenity unless we start to practise some humility. Humility is the bottom line if we are to leave our depression. We must ask that our shortcomings be removed if we are to get beyond our hurting selves into the self that we want to become.

We know that the English word, "humility" comes from the Latin word *humus*, which means the earth. If we are honest and humble we then will be true to ourselves and to others. We will no longer continue to deny the facts about our addiction to sadness, and tell ourselves that the only thing that we need to do is just take some pills and we'll be all right. Pills are fine to take away the pain, and we are thankful that they are there because we need them to help us get back on our feet. But pills cannot remove the reason for the pain nor can they remove our shortcomings. We have to face the truth and admit that somehow I am the cause of my depression. And by our contact with others who also are depressed we can determine some better strategies on how to get through our depression. We can now work on brushing aside any stigma attached to our depression, and admit that right now we are helpless, like the alcoholic who came to AA and said that he had tried every other method of freeing himself from his compulsive behaviour and was now willing to try this twelve-step programme. This programme of recovery has worked for millions who are sober today and who are taking their message of how it was with their life before they began to live and work with the twelve-step programme. They, like all members of twelve-step programmes who are serious about their recovery, can tell people how their lives have changed since they have begun to live the steps.

We learn with time that it is only by springcleaning and admitting our powerlessness that we begin to recover. Now that I humbly admit my shortcomings the Higher Power can begin to work in my life. Without a doubt, it is when we don't want to go to our DA meetings that we really need to be there. It is easy to sit at home and reflect on how bad we are and how bleak and uninviting our future appears to be. But when we become more humble (truthful) and share how we have surrendered our need to be perfect and now can face the truth about ourselves – it is then that we can begin to live.

We notice in step seven that we don't tell God HOW we want Him to remove our shortcomings – we leave that up to Him. This of course takes time, just as it took time to develop our shortcomings or our defects of character. Sometimes we hear some professionals say that people who are depressing themselves shouldn't spend time taking an inventory of their faults or shortcomings because that is what got us here in the first place – namely, dissecting and bashing ourselves for all the bad things we have done and have become. Why would those depressed want to make themselves sadder? The answer to this is that you will not make yourself sadder; you will make yourself healthier as you humbly admit how you have kept yourself locked up in the prison of your depression by any or all of the following: your perfectionism, your anger, anxiety, indecisiveness, feeling always over-whelmed, self-doubts, all or nothing thinking, your pass-ivity and avoidance of getting in touch with your feelings, people pleasing, pessimism towards yourself, lack of feel-ing competent, loss of identity, feeling unconnected to the world, and finally, feeling socially isolated. These are some of the shortcomings that each of us has to look at if we are to live with any amount of freedom. Some of the above are sure to be part of the depressed person's life and thinking. As one person told Dorothy Rowe:

> When I think of all those years I wasted being depressed, I wish I had listened. I wish I'd realized that all I had to do was to say I'd had enough of being put upon and put down, feeling there was something wrong with me. I'd like to go up to the hospital and tell everybody, "You don't have to be like this." Up there nobody every told me that. I'd see those people going on and on being miserable. If I'd have seen some-one like me now, it would have given me hope. (20)

In the group, as well as in our own individual times of reflection, we admit that perfectionism has affected our belief system, which in turn affects the way we feel, with the result that our behaviour acts this belief out in that never-ending cycling and downward feeling of defeat.

We who tend to be perfectionists experience anxiety and/or panic attacks, fearing some vague punishment if we don't produce up to our unrealistic expectations. The perfectionist feels unaccepted by others and by him- or herself.

Sometimes the physical symptoms accompanying perfectionism are stomach problems, overeating and an inability to get to sleep. It's obvious that thinking these perfectionistic thoughts doesn't do us any good. Fatigue is another indicator that something is being overdone and out of whack in our life.

We need humbly to ask God to remove this major shortcoming of needing to be perfect, because we will never be able to accept ourselves unless we admit that we are made of clay like everyone else. No one expects you or me to be some superior human being. Somewhere along in our development, most likely in our early childhood, we got the message that we weren't OK unless we did everything just perfectly. We want to admit the need to be perfect to God and to another human being. We have to tell ourselves that it is OK to fail and to make mistakes. No longer will we accept our past thinking that our worth is based on our ability to produce. This is erroneous thinking!

One makes a choice when making a decision. One of the hard things in a depressed person's life is making a decision. The indecision is what really gets to a person and continually keeps him or her off balance. Usually this indecision is the result of an emotional war going on inside, and both sides war over who will have their way. The more depressed we become the less able are we to muster up the necessary energy to make a decision that will benefit us. I believe that this moral type of inventory is not going to be detrimental to our recovery because it is all about our recovery. We are not intending it to make us feel ashamed but to help us see that if we want to feel better then we have to start to make some changes which are gradual at first. Changing old habits and ways of thinking will with time and work make our personal world a better place to live. Just as the third step states that we made a decision to turn our wills and our lives over to the care of God as we understood Him, we believe that our recovery is about decisions and choices. We have to decide a hundred times daily that we are going to turn our lives and our wills over to the care of God as we understand Him. In time we will feel secure enough to put our depression behind us. In other words, our depression will no longer serve a purpose in our life.

We have to acknowledge humbly that I am the one who is having the harsh and negative thoughts about myself, and that I alone must take responsibility for the feelings that I have about myself. I can't continue to blame others for my depression and still think that I will feel better. Dorothy Rowe says that instead of blaming someone else or making someone else the scapegoat for our problems, we need to put aside blame and guilt and think in terms of responsibilities and connections. What she means here is that when she has dealt with depressed people they seem as though they are carrying the weight of the world and feel responsible for everyone and everything – except their own selves. She says that they see themselves as totally powerless when it comes to their selves. We need to look at what is happening in the here and now and take responsibility for our lives, without living in fear of tomorrow and the hurts of yesterday. Humbly ask God to help you live in the now, even if that means living with the temporary, horrible pain of depression.

People won't change until they have some assurance that when they do change they will be completely happy. They want to have someone promise them that if they decide to change they will have no more problems and will be happy. Dorothy Rowe says that:

This request is based on two assumptions, namely: 1. Anyone who hasn't got my problems has no problems at all (therefore when my present problems disappear I shall have no problems); 2. Happiness is total certainty (therefore unless I know exactly what is going to happen I cannot be happy).(17)

Change is risky and some folks don't want to live with risk – they want life to be completely predictable. But with predictability you pay the price of hopelessness. Hope can exist only when there is uncertainty. You never want anything to change. You want life to be completely under your control.

Pride is not only one of the major sins that we all fall prey to at one time or other in our life, but it is our pride that keeps us from humbly admitting anything at all – namely that I might be the reason that I am depressed. But if you really are sincere in wanting to get out of depression then you have to be ready to let God remove your shortcomings and He will. Sometimes we hear persons who are continually depressed tell how bad they are and that they can't believe anyone could ever love them if they really got to know them. I find that attitude more on the side of pride than humility, because these people are claiming to be special because they are so bad, rather than to be ordinary like everyone else.

In our prison of depression, we at least know what to expect – it's predictable. There is a certain security in knowing you will always feel the same.

Not only will honesty about ourselves help lead us into areas of a meaningful recovery, but it will allow the Higher Power to quicken our spirit as we honestly face one shortcoming after another and gradually root them out of our lives. We have lived so long with this horrible feeling and are so ashamed to tell anyone how bad we have really felt because they would think we were crazy, that we kept this shameful secret to ourselves. It is only in the telling of the truth of ourselves in a humble and courageous fashion that we will be led to new and healing discoveries within. The more active we become in our own recovery and the more that we live for ourselves, the more we are able to throw off our past inertia and begin to go to meetings and share our lives with others. We will slowly gain a new confidence in ourselves and find out that God does want us with others who are depressed and desires to let His power work in our lives. Just as we have been wounded by our family, our church, our society, so we can be healed by the group – namely, the DA group, our new family. It is here that you will find acceptance, nurture and the ability to learn new skills in relating to others. Everyone who is active in the group has already made the decision to turn their lives over to the care of God as they understand Him, and they have admitted that their depression has put their lives out of control. The only thing they have to lose by being a member of DA is their depression.

One member of Alcoholics Anonymous said that "The more meetings you attend, the more people you meet at these meetings, the clearer the steps become. We must learn to walk before we can run."(1) In all changes that have to do with our personality we learn that the change is slow and often painful. In the "letting go" and the surrender that this demands we have to let God do His work in us. This is the part where we must wait on God and let Him do His work in us. This is when we need humbly to let go of our choosing to hang on to depression

for something we don't know anything about. We worried-
ly ask what will happen to me? Will I survive?

We have to let Him do the work. Let Him be in control.
Let Him do it His way and in His time. This is difficult
for those who are depressed and who would rather stay
in their misery than have a challenge to their addiction to
isolation. The seventh step prayer mentions how our
defects of character stand in the way of being useful to
God and our neighbours. God wants to clear away the
debris of those hurts and feelings that continue to keep
us "holed up" in a bubble of self-seeking, self-pity and
fear. The fear is what gets us as we gradually attempt to
emerge into the world of unknown avenues. The old tapes
in our heads keep playing the same old tune – "you can't
be happy!"

In DA we find honest people talking in honest fashion
about how the Higher Power is removing their defects of
character and how they are beginning to see some of their
feelings start to lighten up. The acceptance that they find
among the members of the group is what helps them
relearn the skills necessary to function in their relationships outside the group. The days and hours spent in DA
can help us connect with the world again. Healing is
about being connected. Our connectedness is being
restored, and maybe we never felt connected to a loving
God but instead had felt that our God as we understood
Him was an unmerciful taskmaster who would take away
heaven and our loved ones if we were bad. DA and the
twelve steps help us believe that all we have to do is make
a decision to turn our lives over to Him. He then can
prevent our getting lost along the dead end of blame and
self-pity. The Higher Power will get you focused on the
blocks that you have set up to defeat yourself. He will let
the light in to expose all those areas of your life that have

helped you fear the risk of being you and living life to the fullest.

"When we drew near to Him He disclosed Himself to us!"(1) I believe that this Higher Power, God, will definitely lead you to the happiness that you seek. The closer and more often you turn your mind and heart over to this Higher Power, work the programme and come to meetings, you will gradually feel and see a new change in your life. It will come as long as you present yourself on a regular basis before the Higher Power with your needs. Remember, that to find our way out of depression, I must first admit that I can't get out of depression just by *will power* alone. We know that we can't just snap out of depression, because our whole person, our whole body is involved in this physical numbing of feelings and so we feel disconnected from everything around us. The reason why we have been depressed for so long is not as important as the fact that we admit that we are depressed. Some of the people who come to DA have become depressed only recently due to the loss of a love, loss of self-esteem, loss of a job or family problem. Usually depression results from a loss and some swallowed anger about a painful situation in one's life. DA is also very helpful to persons who feel that they have been depressed all their lives . . . and for the first time are able to put a name on what they have been feeling all these years. Many times a person's depression stems from a childhood loss, such as a parent dying or leaving because of divorce. This has an effect on a child which may continue into adulthood. As has been mentioned elsewhere, losses of significant people early in life continue to live inside us as we grow older in adulthood. Sometimes these manifest themselves as addictive relationships to other people, and the fear of being abandoned in this type of dependent relationship can cause one to be depressed.

We believe that *honesty, openness* and *a willingness* to quit depressing are the basic building blocks of our recovery. To admit our powerlessness and believe that there is a power greater than ourselves is what is going to give my life purpose and hope. And finally we believe that humility is the rock on which each of the twelve steps of DA is based. We can say the prayer

My creator, I am now willing that you should have all of me, good and bad. I pray that You now remove from me every single defect of character which stands in the way of my usefulness to You and my fellows. Grant me strength, as I go out from here to do your bidding.(1)

Helen's Story

I remember being very sad when I was very young, but I really didn't understand that the sadness which I always experienced was called depression. I was sad as a child. I was not too happy to be living. I felt that I was never quite good enough to compete in school, and I always felt that I should leave to someone else whatever we were doing. I suffered on and off with depression throughout school. I felt that I had a loving family, but there was always that depression.

When I went into adulthood I still had that depression. As I got older, the depression got worse. As time went by the people I needed died. They were never there for me to lean on and the depression got worse.

Throughout my life I was always determined to be in control. I had a great need to be in control. I felt weak if I wasn't in control. I guess I thought that if I was in control, complete control, then the feeling that I wasn't quite as good as someone else would pass. I was never satisfied with what I would do. I always thought that I could do better. I was taught to do as well as I could. I guess I was my own worst enemy, but I never expected that from others. I always thought other people were okay; I expected so much from me.

That inner battle went on; the depression went on. I

could always sit down and talk with my mother. She made life so simple. After she was gone, I completely fell apart. I got more and more depressed. I didn't go out and find help because I was too scared. At first I didn't know if there was anyone who could like me. I seemed to be too scared. How could they accept a person like me? Somebody had to accept me the way I was or nobody could help me.

My children were all married and had left home, and I was divorced from my husband. I would come home to that empty house. I wasn't interested in anything. I didn't like television, radio, the video or anything that made a sound. I just wanted to sit quietly in the corner. At the time I was doing it, I didn't realize I was doing this. I was thinking of all the old negative thoughts that were making me so sick. I was not sleeping very much and had chest pains. That went on for a long time but I really didn't care what was wrong. I would think to myself, "You are a worthless person anyway, always have been, don't go to a doctor and take up his time, you're not worth it." Daytime at work was okay, but when daylight came to be night-time, I would just sit in the dark. It was somehow a comfort and it felt good at the time. The only thing I could think was how I made a blunder on the job. "You could have done this or done that at work." I kept telling myself I should have been more friendly on the street to an acquaintance. I kept beating myself over the head about things that happened a long, long time ago. I got to where I wouldn't see people. I would smile at people who came to my home and tell them that I was fine, couldn't be better. You weren't supposed to be rude to people who came to your home. If they find out who I am really, and what I am really, they will discard me completely. If I could tell all this to someone, but why tell it to anyone, who wants to hear it?

Then I finally knew after two years or more of sleepless nights that someone had to help me. I looked up in the back of my phone book and I found a card saying DEPRESSION CENTRE. It had a phone number and that was all. I talked to the man on the other end of the phone. I said to myself this man is too busy to talk with me, but anyway I made that first appointment myself. I made myself go. I thank God that I did. I thank God that I went for help. It was a whole new beginning for me. I wanted to get well so badly. I think people do have to want to change. I went in with the attitude that I have to get well. If there is anything this side of heaven I am going to get it. I had heard things about counsellors that scared me, but this was just all the old negative feelings that caught up with me and boxed me in. I got better and started to think differently. I started to get rid of some of my negative thoughts. I began to feel better and I continued to see Hugh. I started in DA some weeks later.

It has been a year now since I gave up on those negative thoughts that I had over my lifetime. I gave them up one at a time. It wasn't like I dumped them all at once. It was like these people needed to show me a new life and that I can be happy again. In the beginning I thought the old familiar tapes had begun playing again. The old tapes saying I was stupid began to play. But then I would attend DA meetings every week and I would go and find that I could use things that other people said at the meeting which would help me. That it was one place where you could go and be fully accepted for whatever you had to say, and someone else there said they knew exactly what I was feeling. I also began to trust in God, God is my higher power. More and more I turned it over to the

Higher Power and said I can't do these things by myself. I did pray as hard as I could. I prayed every night and I believed that this change was going to happen. I started believing in me. But the wonderful thing was that I began to realize that I was no longer alone. A higher power was going to be there for me. The chest pains soon subsided and I began to sleep again.

You don't get better overnight, but you do get well and you do get much better. I was down in the muck as far as I could go. I had to go and open that door for the first time because there was no other place to go. I had already used up all the hiding places in my life. I still have many problems like anyone else, but if I need sleep very badly I turn the problem over to the Higher Power and go to sleep. I can always pick it up the next morning – somehow it all gets done. Nothing so bad has happened to me. I have trouble trying to figure out what I am exactly supposed to do. I am sure God points me in the right direction but sometimes I miss the message, but it will come to me eventually what God wants for me. All you have to do is reach out and get it. But my faith is stronger now in God than it ever has been in my life because I need that companion in my life. It is there for all of us if we just reach out and take it. It is there for everyone.

Now that I look back and see the way I was and see how I am now, I can't believe that I ever knew that other person. This person is different altogether. I like this person now very much. I am so thankful to the group. They are just wonderful. They are my family. They are my DA family. I also have my church family. It is a wonderful feeling to know that there is a higher power that can help you through these things. At first I thought, "I doubt that very much", when everyone was talking about the Higher Power, peace in my life. I said, "I doubt that very much", and then it happened to me. Every few days the world dumps down on you and beats you down, but that's just life. I always think to myself that there is that extra strength that I didn't have before. I feel that everything is going to be OK with me. I have that peace now myself.

It can't happen overnight. I know what the people who come to DA for the first time feel. When you go through the long weeks and days and give it all you have got, it will happen to you just as it happened to me. There is no magic cure – no magic pill. It is a long process, it will happen and does happen. It is so much better than staying in that dark hole and not getting anything out of life. No longer could I blame this one or that one for causing me pain. I know that it was me that was beating myself up. I was unequipped to handle the problems of my life without the Higher Power, without the tools and material to build the better life.

I also had to get all my priorities straight. I put a lot of importance on things that were not important, like what somebody else might say about me. I was afraid to change, afraid that I would change into a person that would be selfish and uncaring, but it didn't happen that way. I just found a different way to go about it. In getting my priorities straight I discovered that if a person doesn't accept me the way I am, then that doesn't matter as I am going to do the best I can, and if someone else can't handle that, then I am awfully sorry about that, but it has to be. I wanted everyone to approve of me, but they are just not going to do that. I am not going to please everyone. I have got to take care of myself. I was so busy trying to please everyone else that I wasn't taking care of my own needs. At the time I was doing it, I didn't realize that I was doing it. Now I won't deliberately hurt anyone else, but I am going to take care of me too.

Step Eight

Made a List of all Persons we had harmed, and became willing to Make Amends to Them All

One of the dead-end streets that addicted people travel down – often at breakneck speeds – is to blame everyone else for their problems. This indicates an unhealthy mental attitude. In this step eight the founders of AA saw that if we are to get sober and remain that way then we must look around and take stock of people we have harmed. I mean we must take out the paper and pencil and make a list of all those persons whose lives have been made more difficult because of our depression. We might ask how our depression could possibly hurt anyone. To be living with a person depressed is to experience their lows and feel as trapped as they do. If you have been sad and depressed over any length of time just know that it has adversely affected people around you.

Our depression is such that it has kept us at arm's

length and disconnected from other people, friends and family. The first persons on our list that we need to make amends to are those who for whatever reason need our words of forgiveness. This step and the next two (steps nine and ten) have to do with our relationships and the extent to which our depression has damaged our connections between friends and family.

We might want to forgive ourselves for the lack of trust we place in ourselves. After having attended a few more DA meetings we begin to see ourselves in many of the people who share their stories with the group. We start to get connected with the lives of those around us and begin to look inside ourselves, possibly for the first time, and begin to admit to ourselves how we have cut ourselves off from others. We also need to make amends to those whom we have hurt, ignored or in some way separated ourselves from by our depression.

We at this point need to look at the people whom we have hurt by our sadness and general lack of caring. We need to examine the times when instead of being part of the world around us, we decided to withdraw and isolate ourselves in our own little world. We thrive on telling ourselves how bad we are, how imperfect we are and how no one could genuinely care for us. We wallowed in this self-pity and some of us have even tried to take our own lives. We had convinced ourselves that we were worthless and that there was nothing that we could ever do to change our situation.

I thought that my sadness, fear and social isolation affected only me and so I never thought that my depression, irritability and negativity had any direct effect on those around me. I never realized the extent to which my attitudes and compulsive behaviour to sad myself affected others besides myself. But, like all other compulsive behaviour and addictions, it is apparent that our lives affect the lives of others.

Once we begin to recover from this sadness addiction and the false security that this provides we learn that by making a list of those persons whom we have harmed we are now willing to make direct amends to them. But you might ask, isn't this a little embarrassing? Yes, it just might be, but it also will bring you a closer step to staying serene and help you continue your programme of getting beyond a life lived in continual misery and self-pity.

Feeling worthless, hopeless and helpless we somehow blame everyone else for our sadness. We clutch on to our stubborn denial that our life will ever get better or that we can do anything about our own recovery. We need to talk with those people we have harmed by our sadness and show them that we are attempting to change and choose happiness instead of sadness. We can tell them that we want to be different and that we are choosing a life filled with hope instead of a life filled with despair.

The list that we make can include family, co-workers, neighbours and others whom we have touched in any negative fashion. We need to get in touch with how our depression has negatively affected our family and how we have used our addiction to sadness to keep us from getting in touch with the feelings and emotions that we have kept bottled up over the years.

It seems to me that the more we share our story with other members of the DA group, the more we can hear for the first time our own unique story. It is amazing how, when we speak to others about ourselves and our addictions, we begin to loosen up and release in ourselves a new sense of ourselves – a freedom to express our true selves. It is at these times when we discuss our addiction at the DA meetings that we can get first-hand information and feedback on how others are walking free of their sadness and hollowness.

If our identity is based primarily on our sad mood and sense of futility then we need to share this feeling with those we make amends to. Our sadness doesn't exist in isolation. Many times we hear ourselves say that we are "depressives". I personally find this limiting as we are more than just depressed. We never want to assume the identity of being a "depressive" – you might think, act and believe that this is what you will be for the rest of your life. And if we are going to treat depression like any other addiction such as alcoholism, gambling, sexual and love addictions or overeating then why not call ourselves what we are, namely, *sadd*icts. If the alcoholic can recover so can the *sadd*ict. I believe the word *sadd*ict says it better than the word "depressive". The word *sadd*ict promotes the belief that yes, we are addicted to sadness but through the help of the Higher Power, the DA group and the twelve steps I can find a way out of my obsession with sadness. The word "depressive" tends not to promote or provide a sense of hope.

Both alcoholic and *sadd*ict will recover and find that sought-after serenity as long as they continue to keep honest about their addiction and are alert as to how it keeps them from facing the reality of their lives. We know that our health can be compromised by continued negative emotions and feelings about ourselves. Any intense emotion, such as a continual rumination over our personal worthlessness, for example, can over time cause serious physiological damage. Many people say that the doctor has told them that they have a chemical imbalance and this is what causes their depression – *it doesn't cause it* – it continues it. The repetitive negative thoughts about oneself, about one's past and/or future are what cause the physiological changes in the brain chemistry and yes, we then have a chemical reaction. The doctor prescribes the tablets that may reduce brain chemistry deficits and one may start feeling better. Some doctors after prescribing the medication might want to refer you to a counsellor so that you may begin to work out the problems that caused the depression in the first place. When you and I begin to work on our life's journey and start to make this list of people we have resentments against, and begin to forgive them, then this is the beginning of making things right in our life. In fact you might now be feeling better for the first time in your life as you continue to make a conscious effort to take responsibility for your sadness. You realize that you no longer want to stay depressed but instead are willing to risk feeling better (differently). This is taking the risk of being willing to change. When a person stops smoking there is a residue craving for nicotine, and the craving is most painful for the first weeks after quitting the addiction. Gradually over time, and due to being able to say no to the impulse to smoke, you feel stronger and so the painful withdrawal becomes less intense. The same applies to the addiction of depression in that at first it's difficult to stop completely the compulsive repeating of sad thoughts, but with time and working our twelve steps and our active involvement with DA we have the strength to say no to these sad thoughts and begin to choose hope and serenity instead.

In my field of counselling I always tried to get the family of the depressed person into counselling too so that I might help the person see how their depressing them-selves was affecting everyone in the family, including the children. The spouse, if the depressed person was married, always seemed relieved that someone finally could see their viewpoint and understand how they felt and the pain that they too were experiencing. Many times they would tell how their spouse would never do anything and always put things off until they felt better. But they never did feel better! I found much anger and frustration in these relationships, as the spouse was beside himself or herself concerning what to do for their sad partner. They were not only becoming depressed themselves but they were also feeling guilty about the anger they felt when around the depressed person. How, they thought, could they feel all this anger at someone who was supposed to be sick?

Again we must turn to ourselves and begin to examine our own resentments and grudges, which time after time cause us to sink into a stupor of mournful sadness. Many times our resentments are over how badly we were treated as children and how no one really cared how we felt. These resentments become like lead as they keep our steps heavy and burdensome. We can write down all the people who in any way we have hurt by our depression and resentments. We know by painful experience that the depressed person puts a lot of stock in the past and has a tendency to live there. It is precisely here that we need to jog our memories and ask forgiveness of those persons we feel we have hurt.

You might have on your list one of the multitude of organized religions which you blame for all the bad things that have happened to you in the past and which you keep turning over in your mind. You also might want to put on the list a former girlfriend/boyfriend or spouse whom you claim took away all your joy from life, and so you punished them by your continued negativism and angry feelings. When she/he left you lost all reason for living and resent the fact that she/he married someone else. You might want to put your parents, step-parents, brothers and/or sisters on the list as people whom you need to forgive. You might include in this group some minister, priest or rabbi whom you have blamed for your problems. You might also want to ask forgiveness of a child or your children for not getting involved and participating more fully in their lives, because you were stewing in your own feelings of worthlessness and guilt. You discover now how that has prevented you from loving others – especially those in your own family who needed it most from you. You have felt shame for not being what you felt you should have been in life, and for not living up to the expectations of family, friends and employers. You also need to look at how you need to forgive yourself for not being perfect. You might again want to make amends to your parents who demanded something of you that you could never be. We don't blame here – we forgive.

Maybe I need to make amends to my children for making a clean house the number one priority, and never allowing them to give expression to their feelings. Or maybe I was the good daughter or son who never told anyone how I really felt because I was afraid of how my parent(s) would react. Now we might be dredging up all the old feelings of anger and resentment that have been submerged under a mask of kindness and sweetness over the years. We need to voice our anger for having to act like someone that we aren't. I can think of the many women who in therapy begin to get in touch with the times when as little girls they were conditioned to think that good little girls didn't get angry, and so they stuffed and sat upon all these powerful and unpleasant emotions. Feelings that are not expressed can accumulate in our bodies and can't get out until we share them and express them. These stuffed feelings get lodged in our bodies and gradually immobilize us until we feel completely wrung out!

Some have heard all their lives that you shouldn't get angry as Mummy won't love you any more. This makes it quite difficult suddenly to shout out our rage and anger at a world that has made women in general feel less than second-class citizens.

In our depression support groups you can come and begin to let out some of those feelings accumulated over the years, which have taken their toll on our lives making us feel helpless and alone. Many women in our culture seemed to have imbibed a helpless feeling with their mother's milk. As women become aware of their abilities and rights as human beings they begin to experience the freedom that comes from being themselves and throwing aside rules and roles fashioned by men and male minds. Recovery is being able to trust ourselves in exploring ways to feel our emotions.

We can at this time add to the list of people we have harmed and be willing to admit to them how we didn't trust them when they said we were good or said we have this or that ability. One of the hardest things for us to accept is that we might have something good going for us. We feel that people can only love us for what we own or how clean our house is or how much money I make at my job – I believed no one could love me for just me. We really never fully trusted anyone, and that included our God, our religious leaders, our spouses, our children, our best friends.

This step and the next one are the ones that continue our stepping out fearlessly into that brand new world where we daily risk to live with increased hope.

Step Nine

Made direct Amends to
such People wherever possible,
except when to do so would
injure Them or Others

This step is all about self-appraisal. We need to take this inventory and ask forgiveness of the wrongs that we have done to family, friends and others. We are willing to go to any length to win in this battle over depression and feeling down. We need to forgive others and we need to ask forgiveness of those whom we might have injured by our words and actions. And *Alcoholics Anonymous* points out. ". . . (t)his is not an end in itself. Our real purpose is to fit ourselves to be of maximum service to God and the people about us."(1)

We need to look at our relationships now and in the past and see whom we need to ask forgiveness from for our past wrong actions. There is something therapeutic about seeking forgiveness and being forgiven for past wrongs. It is a fact that once we clear the air of past wrongs there is released in us a lightness of spirit that can only be experienced by letting go of an old hurt, guilt feeling or sense of shame.

Many persons think that asking for forgiveness would be too embarrassing . . . yes it might be embarrassing, but it will also be a new beginning for you as you give an old resentment or grudge the boot. Just as in the past our resentments against another gave us the necessary ammunition that we felt we needed to stay in our depression, so here too.

We need first of all at this point to continue with the list of people whom we had hurt. This list must be prayed over and reflected upon so that we can do the proper springcleaning and have the peace and the serenity promised to those who choose to take responsibility for their own actions. Reaching out to those that we might have harmed by making amends is the *only* way to continue on the path of recovery. The shame that finally leaves us will free us for the full and firm conviction that I have a right to be on this earth and yes I know now that even though I am not perfect I still can be who I want to be and that's fine.

Fight or flight might be our dilemma as we begin to put some teeth into our recovery programme. We might want to flee from those persons we have harmed instead of facing them and making amends to them. This fight or flight emotion applies with equal force to those memories of childhood that might be too painful for us to face, and so we flee them – we find it difficult to get in touch with them. We also might be tempted to fight for our personal pride at times, falsely thinking that we really don't need to make amends to anyone and that we are just fine the way we are.

It is true that we won't ever have any peace and serenity

until we make peace with those around us. We want to take a close look at those people who make us feel so small and worthless when we are around them or think of them from our past. We also need to make amends to those persons who made us feel that we were small and worthless . . . made us feel shame about ourselves.

As you continue in your recovery process using these twelve steps you might already find people from the past coming to your mental screen. Well, you say, I have been good and I have tried to be perfect so why am I still so miserable and unhappy? The reason that you are so unhappy is because you are trying to be perfect, but you never know when you reach perfection as you always have one more line to cross before you become the perfect person that you are struggling so hard to become.

Depression is so often a refuge from having to live out our life. And it is only when we feel that we can live with a fair degree of unpredictableness in our lives that we move out of our isolation into the real world. So often our depression hides behind a mask of superficial friendliness – with people never aware of the deep pain that we feel inside. The risk is in moving out of isolation into contact with other depressed people. We know now that it is the expression of our feelings that gets us free. It is the telling and the admission of our powerlessness over our depression that makes us move ever so slowly out of the deep pit of darkness and sadness. So often when we are able to make amends we feel that part of the prison wall begins to crumble and we begin to see the light of day. We discover a way out! We find that our forgiveness of others frees us and brings us one more step into the peace of serenity. Getting free is in saying that we alone are responsible for our compulsive retreat from life when we run up against some stressful situation. And the more we

study and hear about addictive personalities and
behaviour, the more we learn about ourselves and how
we have anaesthetized ourselves against any possible feelings of pain, hurt or anger by sadding ourselves and
keeping to ourselves.

So often we perceive other people as being stronger
than we are. We see people more cheerful and happy
than we are, and so we are sure that they cannot be really
all that happy when I am feeling so miserable. I need now
to make amends to myself for my fear that I might never
smile or laugh again. This is the beginning of the end of
our sadding – to admit our reluctance to choose life
instead of those familiar feelings of sadness.

I know that a number of people who are first introduced
to the twelve-step programme wonder what their sadness
has to do with this spiritual programme of twelve steps
that originated for alcoholics. I might be depressed but I
am surely not a drunk. Sometimes you will hear a new
member of the group say that they never committed any
wrong against anyone, and so why do they need to make
amends? For many persons the loss of a love, the death
of a spouse, the end of a lifetime career can produce a
spiralling sense of despair in people whose whole lives
have centred on someone or something outside themselves. Many times these very same people might be co-
dependent on others – that is, they are more concerned
about someone else's feelings than their own. Their lives
are lived in someone else rather than being lived in their
own self. When that other person is lost they feel lost and
abandoned. This is precisely the point – the need to make
amends for erroneously thinking that someone else can
satisfy all their wants and desires. In making amends we
begin to take responsibility for our thoughts and feelings,

and when these have hurt others we need to do something about them.

The depression is so bad at times that we feel no one would ever understand how we feel – unless of course they have been there. We just have about given up on God, Church, family and friends as allies on our behalf. We feel resentments and anger toward people for not feeling more sympathetic toward our never-ending sadness. We feel that people aren't kind and don't treat us with the same respect that they do other people, such as the diabetic, insomniac or arthritic person. Most people don't want anything to do with us because they get tired of our moaning, groaning and pessimistic way of looking at life. Why shouldn't they? Life is tough enough without having to be subjected to another's gloom and doom. But this is the place where we recognize the difference between ourselves and others, and of course we think our lot is always the worst of all. This self-pity never brings us into any personal sense of peace but has just the opposite effect in that it helps perpetuate the myth that *depression floats in like a dark cloud over which we have no control*. We need to tell spouse, family and friends that we want to start again and begin to take charge of our lives and start to chip away at our sadness. We won't blame our need to sadden ourselves on what my wife/husband did or did not do for us, or what a friend said or didn't say. We finally have to take the bull by the horns much like the recovering alcoholic, overeater, gambler, smoker, and admit that it is I that have the problem and that it no longer does any good to blame others for my problem. Once I admit that I am addicted to depressing myself then I can begin to walk through the door of the prison that binds me. I must realize the fact that my depression will only get worse unless I put a stop to all the thinking, feeling and acting out behaviour that keeps me perpetually locked into my sadness.

Many times the people we would like to make amends to are dead and long gone – except that they live in our memories. What we can do here is tell our friends about our need to make amends to them and with that know that we have done the best thing that we can do, judging by the circumstances. Many times our lives have been traumatized from the very beginning of childhood when one or other parent abandoned us, and we felt that loss deeply so that the sadness of a childhood never lived continues to motivate our every action. Our inability to live with any amount of trust makes it difficult to trust a Higher Power that it too won't abandon us or punish us like an early caretaker did when we were children.

Institutions have many times incurred our wrath and we fear them because they are all-powerful and can hurt us if we are not careful, and so we watch our thoughts and actions. In fact we have to be very sure that we are always walking the line with religious institutions because they seem to have a direct line from God; this in itself makes us even more aware of our weakness and vulnerability and shame – just as when we were children. We hate to admit it but we have had angry and hateful thoughts against these representatives of God who go about so smug and haughty, casting into hell those not on God's special guest list destined for heaven. These feelings that we never share with others are not able to be brought into the open where they are given the light of day.

We also want to caution about rushing headlong into some sort of compulsive need to seek out all those people we need to make amends to. If we go too fast we might just make ourselves more depressed, as we find that not everyone is as interested in hearing you make amends as you are. As you continue to get in touch with your feelings, stuffed and frozen over the years, you will find that some people might not trust your good intentions and suspect your recent conversion. Some would rather hold off their personal judgements as to whether or not you are really wanting to change and have a more hopeful attitude to life. Don't be too disappointed then if some people aren't as thrilled as you are about your newfound attitudes.

One of the better ways to make amends is to commit yourself on a daily basis to helping other members of the DA group find peace and serenity. It is when we each begin to take responsibility and control over our lives and quit blaming the weather, other people, ourselves, institutions, or our jobs for our sadness that we begin to feel more whole and in recovery.

> Our real purpose is to fit ourselves to be of maximum service to God and the people about us. . . .
>
> Yes, there is a long period of reconstruction ahead. We must take the lead. A remorseful mumbling that we are sorry won't fill the bill at all. We ought to sit down with the family and frankly analyse the past as we now see it, being very careful not to criticize them. Their defects may be glaring, but the chances are that our own actions are partly responsible. So we clean house with the family, asking each morning that our Creator show us the way of patience, tolerance, kindness and love.(1)

Many times each day we pray that the Higher Power manifest itself in us and our lives. We become more like a plate glass window where the light of God's grace continues to shine through us and in our lives. The Higher

Power is going to make a new path for us to walk as long as we remain in conscious contact with His love, wisdom and guidance.

Step Ten

Continued to take

Personal Inventory

and when we were wrong,

promptly admitted it

As we continue to keep ourselves free of the thoughts that imprison us ever more tightly with our depression, we begin to recognize that this power greater than ourselves can and will restore us to sanity. What this breaks down to is that we learn to surrender to this Higher Power as it helps us remove our character defects, enlarges our circle of friendships by our active participation in the DA group, and helps us take a daily inventory of the times when we needed to make amends to others or to ourselves.

Webster's New World Dictionary (27) says that the word *inventory* means "an itemized list or catalogue of goods, property, etc.; esp., such a list of the stock of a business, taken annually." We continue to take inventory during our day and see whether we have not dealt honestly with past hurts, angry feelings, guilt, bitterness, fear, shame, boredom, stress, poor diet, too little or too much sleep, pessimism, rigidity, dwelling in the past, worrying about the future, feeling insecure and not trusting, feeling misunderstood, and finally the possible use of drugs, including the drug of alcohol. We look at this list and work on a particular character defect and use it as a discussion lead for one of our twelve-step depression group meetings. This is an inventory and it is not taken to make us feel sad but to help us see that it is only in naming the enemy that we can free ourselves from what has held us captive in the past. These are what has built our wall of depression in the past. Call these character defects the bricks that have been used to imprison ourselves in our isolation and confining lifestyle.

For us who have experienced depression over a long time we need to examine whether our sadness comes from "feeling sorry" for ourselves or for some other reason. Sometimes we need to ask ourselves: Is self-pity getting in the way of my recovery? If we think that it is we then need to look at the basic case of our "feeling sorry" for ourselves. Many times we find that a resentment over a past injustice to ourselves is the culprit – or maybe it is something that we have done in the past that we feel we can't or haven't forgiven ourselves for. Sometimes we feel that we haven't been treated fairly, and that makes us continue to feel sad. Also, as we have mentioned frequently before in this work, our sadness may go back to our childhood, resulting from a traumatic situation such as a parent dying, divorcing or abandoning us. Many times just being willing to face this will enable us to process the mourning of a lost childhood, a lost parent or a lost self-identity as a person. We need to do the grief work and mourn this loss in our early life. And so grieving a loss goes through a number of predictable stages and these stages must be experienced if one is to experience a life free of the sadness that might have been hurting for many years.

Many times persons depressed find that the more they get in touch with their feelings, painful as that might be, the more they need to remain with the feelings and really *feel* them. This is the beginning of getting free from their tyranny. We have to get in touch with our feelings of anger, sadness, and the fact of our denial that we have even experienced the fierce feelings of rejection so early in life. There may be some covered-over rage resulting from this unpleasant childhood experience. It's amazing to hear people say that as children they never had a birthday party. We also know that sadness, guilt, shame and a few other losses coming at one time in our life can slowly push us over the line as we find ourselves overwhelmed with stress and feelings of defeat. It's this subtle feeling of being out of control that brings deepening sadness until we finally become immobilized.

Many times just writing down what you are feeling will help you get rid of the pain of that particular feeling. Also, when you speak to someone about how you are experiencing an unpleasant feeling then others can and will be there with you through the pain. Many persons who are in recovery keep a *feelings* journal in which they list the various feelings that they experience from one time to another during their day. It's wise to try to stay with these unpleasant feelings and sort out where they are coming from and how we caused them. Many times when we describe what we feel we begin to release in ourselves the "stuckness" that keeps us in a mood of hopelessness.

Denial and rationalization, both forms of defence

against getting in touch with our compulsion to sad ourselves, need to be eliminated if we are to live life with
hope and start to relish the unpredictability of it all. If
you really are working on the programme you will begin
to see that your recovery is your choice. I can't make you
happy. *You* have to choose to be happy.

Many times we who depress ourselves find that we
have placed a wide gulf between what we are and what
we would like to be. We have such high standards that
we can never reach them, so that we fall back into despair
time after time, which gives credence to the fact that we
really are bad and worthless. We are always wanting to
be the controller. I like what Dorothy Rowe says:

> This desire for perfect control, of the environment and
> of oneself, is based on a profound mistrust of the con-
> troller. Because you see yourself as bad, you cannot
> trust yourself to be. Because you cannot trust yourself
> to become, to allow yourself to grow as a plant grows. (17)

Many times the fear of letting go is a problem for the
compulsive person addicted to his/her sadness.

One of the many beneficial aspects of living out the
twelve-step programme is that we can take a daily inventory of our lives, and we promptly need to admit when
we are wrong. This takes some courage because once you
believe that you are perfect it's difficult to admit that you
need to make amends.

We come to believe that if we do consider ourselves
bad and worthless we just know that no one can really
love us or accept us. We just know, the more we look at
ourselves and our few remaining relationships, that we
really aren't accepted – people just put up with us.

  . . . there is one great advantage about seeing yourself

as helpless and in the power of others. You don't have to be responsible for yourself. Other people make all the decisions and when things turn out badly you can blame other people. And things always turn out badly. You know this. That's why you always expect the worst. (17)

Responsibility is the name of the game in recovery and it is here that we need to focus our attention. As we get into a discussion with other people who are depressed – much like ourselves – we see that they talk about feeling better while at the same time acting on their own behalf. These people who are doing better are also talking about taking charge of their lives and doing things for themselves instead of constantly trying to please others. In fact at DA meetings the recovering people often delight at how assertive they are becoming now that they have gained a sense of mastery over their lives. They also are committed to their own recovery. People who want to change begin to swallow their pride and ask for help. They begin to get in touch with their feelings and feel! This is truth and this is getting in touch with one's best self.

As you well know, when we say we are wrong we create an area of uncertainty . . . if you cannot tolerate uncertainty then you cannot afford to admit that you are wrong. Absolute certainty may appear to you to be a wonderful thing, giving complete security, but have you ever considered that if you want absolute certainty you must give up freedom, love and hope. (17)

This seems to be the main fear for us when depressed, namely, that we won't have our world in our complete control. I think this is where we need to talk to members of our group or we need promptly to admit that we were wrong. The group is the best forum of peers where we can express our deepest fears about losing control and not try to force the world to be as we feel it should be.

Resentments also have a powerful way of getting us sad as we remember all the hurts that have been part of our day and our lives. We can stay in our addiction and build a museum filled with the skeletons of our past hurts, or we can face them, deal with them and move on in the process of our recovery. We need to deal face to face with all our old hurts and then name them and remove them from our lives once and for all. We need to hand them over to the Higher Power and let its desire move them where it will.

We need to get in touch with those feelings from our early childhood days and try to remember when we made ourselves sad and what situation today makes us feel sad. There sometimes is a connection between the two. We know this return to early childhood feelings is one of the best ways to get a beginning in our self-healing. We can talk about how we felt about our mother and father, and how our relationship with them was lived out in childhood. Can we connect with any early childhood event that upon reflection makes us feel sad? Usually this childhood event with its feeling of shame, sadness or guilt is reactivated whenever we come upon a similar incident in our present adult life. Is there some fear of authority figures in our present life? Do we fear other people's anger? What makes us cringe when we feel our feelings will be hurt? These questions about our early childhood and these unpleasant early life experiences still live in our flesh today. It is good when we get in touch with our sadness today, find out what triggers it and then try to go back and see whether the present sadness reminds us of something we felt sad about a long time ago. This is one other road that can lead us out of our sadness.

A member of our group said that her father was very authoritarian and strict. She said that she was always trying to please him and do the best she could with everything he wanted. She said that she could never do things well enough to please him. Even today she still tries to please others, but because of her perfectionistic nature finds herself always inadequate and never satisfied with herself. This produces a feeling of loss as she feels guilty over losing control over those situations in which she wants to excel. She also feels resentments towards other people as they never seem to notice all her outstanding qualities.

Sometimes persons tell us that they get sad for no reason at all – all of a sudden they just feel down and don't know why. Many times after reflecting upon this sudden rush of sadness they realize that it has to come from somewhere and they might as well take responsibility for it and deal with it. One of the best ways to deal with a feeling, especially the unpleasant ones, is to stay with it, feel it and see what it is trying to say to you. When we run from it we lose. Granted, this won't be easy and you might not find the source of the sudden sadness at the first glance, but in time you can feel it, deal with it and then discard it. The more you ruminate about how sad you are and then how bad you are for being so sad, the more you have begun the downward spiral into physically feeling weak and hopeless. This is the time to call a friend or a member of the group. Just say, "Hey, I'm feeling sad and here is the reason why I think I am feeling sad – what do you think?" More times than not your sad feelings will melt away.

But you want absolute certainty and you have too much pride to admit that you could be wrong. You take pride in seeing yourself as essentially bad; you take pride in not loving and accepting other people; pride in the starkness and harshness of your philosophy of life; pride in the sorrows of your past and the blackness of your future; pride in recognizing the evil of anger; pride in not forgiving; pride in your humility; pride in your high standards; pride in your sensitivity; pride in your refusal to lose face by being rejected; pride in your pessimism; pride in your martyrdom; pride in your suffering. (17)

The basic premise about ourselves that has to be faced is that if we truly do see ourselves as bad and worthless then we have to get up off our backs and begin to forgive ourselves and humbly share that we no longer want the misery of our depression. We want to take a risk and face our pride, and work at changing ourselves. Dorothy Rowe's list of prides really takes the steam out of anyone wanting to feel sorry for themselves.

The real risk is when that first inkling comes that because of your active and regular work in the twelve-step depression group you begin to feel a small bit of serenity growing inside you. This is what scares us all. Our guilt, our shame, our losses in life, have almost completely shut down our sense of spontaneity and playfulness, so that we are afraid of the new way we are feeling. Our first thought is that it won't and can't last. That is when we need to face the fear – stay with it and it will flee. As long as you stay with these unpleasant feelings, keep working on yourself at meetings and just tell yourself that you can beat these negative attitudes about yourself, your future and your world, you can start to rebuild.

At this time, call a friend and tell them you need help rebuilding. Instead of allowing your defects of character to imprison you, you are now using those bricks to build a bridge between you and those other members of the group who want to free themselves from the isolating feelings of sadness and hurt.

"Promptly" means at once, and this is especially good for all of us, because when we are depressing we like to go off and ruminate and sad ourselves as to how guilty and bad we are. We need to turn this around so that instead of beating ourselves over the head we need "promptly" to admit that we are sadding ourselves and so free ourselves from the cycle of sad thoughts and begin to distract ourselves by engaging in some positive and pleasurable activity on our own behalf. "Promptly" also means to express a feeling as soon as you feel it. In the past we had the tendency to keep it locked up in ourselves and it got stuck, frozen and unattended to. So feel safe to express what you are feeling, and take credit for its being *your* feeling, that it doesn't belong to someone else. People stress that when you feel something say, "I feel mad" or "I feel happy" or "I feel upset". The point here is that just saying "I" makes a big difference in how you feel. If you say "You make me angry" or "You make me sad" or "You make me upset" this only misplaces the source of your feeling. You need to take full responsibility for how you feel – you can't blame it on anybody else.

Promptly forgive ourselves! Promptly tell a friend, DA group member, co-worker, spouse, that you are now trying to live one day, one hour at a time and are depending on the Higher Power to give you the courage to risk thinking hopeful thoughts which have the power to lead yourself back into the community, the family and among friends. Develop a *gratitude attitude* and thank God for today! This day is all we have. Get involved in your own healing. Start to take on the attitude that if other people can make it then so can I. It's true – you can make it if you follow this programme.

Human beings are never quite alike, so each of us, when making an inventory, will need to determine what his individual character defects are. Having found the shoes that fit, he ought to step into them and walk with new confidence that he is at last on the right track. (3)

Sharlene's Story

I am writing this information with the hope that it will help anyone who is suffering from "depression" brought on by stress, anxiety, loneliness, physical or mental emotions, death, insecurity, etc.

I am a thirty-four-year-old single female, who has been suffering from depression for a long time. Most of my depression was brought on by feelings of insecurity, not being able to express my inner feelings, being controlled by a dominating parent, loneliness, stress (workaholic), anxiety attacks (related to work and everyday pressures of living), too much sleep, nervousness, lack of motivation, being tired all the time, sadness, weight gain, digestive problems, a feeling of being trapped, self-consciousness, not trusting myself, dreams of dying but yet managing to come back to life (a little hard to understand), withdrawal from family, loss of interest in meeting with the opposite sex, etc.

It seemed that I was living in another world until one of my parents gave me a phone number to *Depressed Anonymous*. I have been in private counselling with Hugh Smith, I go to *Depressed Anonymous* meetings and I have also purchased the book *Depression: Here is a way out!* These tools have helped me find a way to live without being depressed. Also, most important of all, the twelve steps mentioned in the book have made me understand that God (my Higher Power) will give me strength to deal with my depression and get on with my life and be happy with myself.

The book, with its twelve steps, has taught me that I am not alone, and that I am not the only one who is suffering from depression. It has taught me to believe more in my Higher Power and to let Him handle my depression.

I read the book, go to counselling and attend the DA meetings (the meetings are a must, I need them to survive). The support group's members help each other by listening, talking, expressing their feelings, and give support and ideas on how to cope with depression. By letting my Higher Power help me, I am beginning to feel free from depression. I am not so nervous and tensed up, my Christian inner faith is getting stronger, I am not so stressed out and I am beginning to get confidence within myself. I still have a little trouble with sleep pattern and I am getting some motivation back. I have learned how to handle anxiety, by taking deep breaths when I am nervous or troubled; this was suggested by my therapist. I also am learning how to stand up for myself!

It seems as if you are discovering a new way of living and new feelings and emotions. All these new tools have helped me and will continue to do so. They also taught me not to dwell on my past, to live life one day at a time and to look towards the future but not live there. It will take me a long time to deal with depression, but I am glad that these tools are available. Life can be good for a change! Please DON'T GIVE UP!

Step Eleven

Sought through Prayer and

Meditation to improve our

Conscious Contact with God

As We Understood Him,

Praying only for Knowledge

of His Will for us and the

Power to carry that out

With our compulsion to sad ourselves, much like the alcoholic's urge to medicate him- or herself with alcohol, we need daily to turn our wills over to God and ask for the Higher Power's guidance. Eventually it is the conscious contact with this loving God that sets us free from the need to sad ourselves.

All of us who are substance-addicted (compulsive over-eating; alcohol; cocaine; prescription medications) or pro-

cess-addicted, i.e., addicted to a behaviour (the workaholic; sex; gambling; depression) know that in order to free
ourselves from the intoxicating experience we have first
to want to give it up and live without it. We best do this
one day or one hour at a time. Don't say you will quit a
self-destructive behaviour for one year and then see how
you do. No, try to live one day at a time – it's a lot easier.
As someone once said, if you want to eat an elephant the
best way to do it is one bite at a time. We know from past
experience that our sobriety, our disappearance of sadness
is due to letting go, admitting my powerlessness over my
sadness and turning it over to my Higher Power and
letting it take care of my sadness. I can't do anything to
remove my compulsive behaviour until I choose to live
without it.

When we are especially depressed it's hard to keep our
mind on things such as prayer, but with continued effort
and practice we can come to believe that whatever we are
doing it just might be better than sitting in our own pool
of self-pity. If we haven't ever been big on "organized
religion" we have a good chance that this new approach
to being with God is much less judgemental, and that this
God of the twelve steps is much more accepting than
other concepts of God that we might once have held.
Sometimes we have found that our religious background
has filled us with a large amount of crippling guilt, shame
and hopelessness rather than the complete acceptance
that we will receive from our Higher Power.

Praying means to ask for something. We ask that we
might let God take over our lives since we have admitted
that we are powerless over our sadding of ourselves and
that our lives have become unmanageable. As it says in
Alcoholics Anonymous, "I saw that it was my LIFE that was
unmanageable – not just my drinking." I believe there is

much wisdom in that short statement, and it is one that I want to reflect upon. The fact that we have pretty much shut ourselves off from the world is not a very sane thing to do when one of our human species' major characteristics is being a social creature.

Our continual sadding ourselves pushes us away from any form of pleasant interaction with others and continually builds the wall higher for our depression. This is the purpose of our continually making conscious contact with our God as we understand Him. I do believe, and I speak from my own experience, that the Higher Power respects our surrender and our letting it take charge of our lives. It is amazing how in our recovery our feelings start to thaw out, we feel some emotions, and the healing begins. For us who are depressing ourselves we can learn that the best way to break free from this chronic sadness is just to admit that we are responsible for our sadness and then pray to God as we understand Him that we want to be serene and happy. We just pray to be set free, and gradually, with small steps and subtle changes taking place inside ourselves, we feel a change occurring.

Every so often we come into contact with a person, place or circumstance that causes us some uncomfortableness and we start to withdraw into the comfort of our depression. It is here that we have dumped our trust of the Higher Power and choose the comfort of our sadness instead.

After falling back into our old comfortable habit of depressing ourselves we then realize we have got ourselves right back where we started – depressed and feeling isolated. We realize that all we have is today. As *Alcoholics Anonymous* points out:

The poorest person has no less and the wealthiest has

no more – each of has but one day. What we do with it is our own business; how we use it is up to us individually. (1)

I remember Fred on his first visit to DA. He said that he had been depressed all his life. The group listened to Fred, and of course for the most part Fred said he didn't have the foggiest notion what all this talk of God had to do with his sadness and how it was supposed to help him. But it was the pain of Fred's depression that brought him back time after time to the meetings, and he started not only to feel better but he began to look better. Then as he heard more about the twelve steps he saw that he could trust this Higher Power, and that maybe the depression that had been such a lifetime companion was not for him anymore. Fred took the plunge, came to believe that a power greater than himself could restore him to sanity – and it did just that. Fred said he didn't need this depression any more, got busy making amends to family, friends and co-workers for being such a negative person, and began to take inventory where he needed to springclean his house. In time Fred began to reach out to others in the group, and he began to understand how he had become like many others in the group, a *sadd*ict. Depression for many was an addiction to sadness. The only way out of Fred's addiction was to let go of it, admit his life was unmanageable and start to work on himself and his character defects. Fred still keeps coming back to the meetings to share his story with others on the *how* of his recovery. He talks about the way it was before DA and the way it is now since he has been working the steps and handing his life over to the Higher Power.

Yes, Fred is tempted to sad himself now and again, but with his dependence on the Higher Power he no longer falls under the compulsion of giving in to the sadness. He is finding that he can choose to be happy, and it is in his daily prayer and meditation times that he feels led by the Higher Power for the day ahead.

AA says that honesty means telling yourself the truth. Also the AA pioneers believed that the Higher Power was at anyone's behest as long as they at least made an effort to contact it:

> We found that God does not make too hard terms with those who seek him. To us, the Realm of Spirit is broad, roomy, all inclusive; never exclusive or forbidding to those who earnestly seek. It is open, we believe, to all men [and women]*.

We believe that to be conscious is to have been able first of all to listen to someone or something that expresses God's desire to free us from our misery as soon as we are willing to turn our minds and our wills over to Him. Somewhere along the way we were convinced that the only safe way to make this life bearable and predictable was continually to sad ourselves, withdraw into our little shell and make sure our own small world was completely under our control. It was a perfect little world this world of ours. It was dark, gloomy and painful – but at least we knew what we had. It is this predictableness that makes life inescapably hell for all of us, even though we'd rather have this than the total surprise of living.

The more we are being led by the Higher Power the more we will be alert to the signals that something positive is beginning to work for us in our life. As we become more desirous of making conscious contact with the Higher Power, the more peace and serenity start to flow

* The language of AA is very sexist, which Hugh deplores.

into our lives. We soon experience a peace that we have never experienced before, and we find that we want more of it as we daily make up our mind to get into contact with the Higher Power. This prayer and meditation, or *P and M* as people in the group call it, makes us ever more aware that it is this spiritual approach that makes our depression less and less of a negative force to be reckoned with in our lives.

Just sitting back and relaxing is a difficult thing to do when we are depressed, but if we want to have the Higher Power work in our lives then we have to quieten ourselves and listen often to its promptings. Listen then and pray. Pray that you might free this sadness in yourself as you continue to work the steps of this programme. The more you live with a *gratitude attitude* the more you will see that life is worth living and that you can live with the unpredictable. Life is supposed to be unpredictable and the reason why it is is that each of us lets God's power unfold in our lives. The more conscious and aware we are of its operating in our universe, the more serenity we have in our lives. We believe that as we take a daily inventory and really work at getting in touch with God then God will reciprocally get in touch with us. It won't be long until our meditation will produce in us a feeling that God is guiding our lives and that His love is putting us back on our feet. We are finding that we want to risk testing out our wings and so we try to live one day at a time and forget about the hurts, fears and pain of yesterday, or the anxious moments that we might face tomorrow. The members of the group call these the *what if's — what if* this happens or *what if* that happens, etc. The Higher Power is only today, it's not yesterday or tomorrow. It lives now. It lives in our hearts and all it wants and desires is that we make contact with it, and then its force will unfold as time continues. With time it will manifest itself, in our minds and hearts.

We only desire God's will for us. How often in the past was I scared to turn my will over to God and let Him do with me as He willed. No way! I wasn't going to have God take over my life and take away all my control. Who knows, He might send me to some God-forsaken island somewhere to talk about God. I wouldn't dare turn over my free will to anything like that. I wanted to stay in control, and the way to do that was by not turning my will over to anyone, especially God. This does say something about our feelings about God, doesn't it? – namely, that we have received the freedom to make ourselves miserable if we like by not trusting, or we can trust and start to work our way out of the darkness of our depression. It is completely up to us, if we so choose. We pray for the knowledge of His will and the power to carry it out. This is another big sentence. The way to pray for the knowledge of His will is continually to make amends to those that we have hurt and promptly to ask forgiveness. There is no room in our recovery for holding on to resentments – this just throws us into sadness and isolation and keeps us in our compulsion to repeat our addictive lifestyles. We continue to feel slights by others as the greatest rejection, and of course this causes us to sad ourselves even more.

We find that no one need have difficulty with the spirituality of the programme. Willingness, honesty and open-mindedness are the essentials of recovery. But these are indispensable. . . .

There is a principle which is a bar against all information, which is proof against all arguments and which cannot fail to keep a man in everlasting ignorance – that principle is contempt prior to investigation. (1)

We can see from this then that persons who have at least the desire to stop their compulsive behaviour to depress can have a chance by following this twelve-step recovery programme. This God-consciousness is what makes the programme of *Depressed Anonymous* work and is at its very core.

We wish to say that any alcoholic capable of honestly facing his problem in the light of our experience can recover, provided he does not close his mind to all spiritual concepts. He can only be defeated by an attitude of intolerance or belligerent denial. (1)

Steps Two and Three, like Step Eleven, are concerned with our wills being in God's will. We should seek, as a priority, a knowledge of His will for us. But the recovery is up to you. You have to be willing and admit that your life is unmanageable – your sadness is out of control. You are honest enough to admit that your pride is blocking you from choosing to get you undepressed.

As it says in *Alcoholics Anonymous*, if someone wants to know *how* the programme works it is *H* for honesty, *O* for open-mindedness, and *W* for a willingness.

Alcoholics Anonymous finds that just a willingness to believe is enough to start a person's programme of sobriety. The desire to free myself from the pain of my sadness becomes greater than the hold that the sadness of the depression has over me.

We also believe that we *saddicts* 'are like men [women] who have lost their legs; they never grow new ones.' (1) We have to conclude that since our depression and sad thoughts are getting progressively worse over the course of time, we then have to admit that our feelings are out of control and that we need help.

I very much like the whole spiritual orientation of the twelve-step way of life – and just because we are a spiritual programme doesn't mean that we are denying the importance of other religious organizations or faiths. I feel that the greatest gift I have ever received is to know that I have an addictive compulsion to depress myself – it is this reality that brought me into the fellowship of DA. It is here that I came in contact with and found a non-judgemental God who cared for me so much that He was willing to wait for me to contact Him.

> The central fact of our lives today is the absolute certainty that our creator has entered into our hearts and lives in a way which is indeed miraculous. He has commenced to accomplish those things for us which we could never do by ourselves. (1)

There is a complete transformation in our lives that begins to take place when all our old ideas are replaced by new, fresh and life-giving ideas. One can become a new person here.

One remembers the prayer of St Francis where he prays to be a channel of God's grace. This is where we come in. Those of us in the programme want to be a force for good in this world, and what greater good can you do for the world than to tell people depressed how being open to the will of God has helped free you of depressed thoughts and feelings? Also by choosing to re-kin ourselves by developing new friendships with others in the DA group we gradually get in touch with the frightened small child inside us. We can begin to get in touch with childhood hurts and quit looking forever for mother and father figures to approve of us and affirm us. Our addiction to getting others' approval begins to wither as we share our story with our new family, the twelve-steps group. We begin to re-parent our child inside and gradually we work through our feelings of shame and sadness. Remember, we don't want to tell God how to run our life. We just want to pray that God will do with us as He wills.

Meditation is getting still inside and listening to the voice and guidance of God. We are very active in meditation even though we let God speak to us. We are receptive to His every prompting of wisdom and love. We have no desire but to desire His will. We are no longer dependent on our will, but His will is what guides us.

Before the day begins we first thank God for the privilege of doing His will today and the time that He has given us. We just ask for the courage to carry out His will in our lives this day. We pray for the serenity that comes from surrendering our will to God's. We need to keep our life simple. We need to take it easy and not get over-involved and overwhelmed by countless duties and concerns. The enormity of life will throw us back into depression unless we start to live with more wisdom and circumspection. Each morning during our meditation we ask that the "Creator show us the way of patience, tolerance, kindliness and love." (1)

We think about the twenty-four hours ahead when we wake up, and attempt to live the day in honesty and peace. We ask God to ward off thoughts of self-seeking, dishonesty and false motives. And as AA says, when we are faced with indecision about something we then ask God for inspiration and we let go of struggling for an answer. *Alcoholics Anonymous* says that you will be surprised at how the right answers will come after we have practised this way of living. It also comes to pass that our hunches are more right than wrong. We also pause throughout the day when we are fearful, puzzled or anxious. We pray to the Higher Power for which direction to take. I like this suggestion the best when AA says that "we constantly remind ourselves we are no longer running the show, humbly saying to ourselves many times each day 'Thy will be done'." We are then in much less danger of excitement, fear, anger, worry, self-pity, or foolish decisions. We become much more efficient. We do not tire so easily, for we are not burning up energy foolishly as we did when we were trying to arrange life to suit ourselves. By coming to the meetings and admitting our addictions we finally get in touch with those emotions that have all but shut down from an early time in our lives, when to feel hurt too much. We now have the chance to let these feelings get displayed and expressed in the supportive and trusting environment of our newly chosen family of the DA group.

Our feelings expressed and positively received by the group allow us then to focus on the way we think about ourselves, and make it possible for us to parent ourselves instead of continually seeking out the lost unavailable parent in the guise of multiple sexual relationships, alcohol, gambling, and any of the many other compulsions that are used to fill the void in our lives.

Practising the programme enables us to be led by the Higher Power to do the most good that we can and which He wants us to do.

The beautiful thing about God is that He is simple. There are not parts to God – no body, mind and soul. We see God as a oneness and are only praying for knowledge of His will and the power to carry it out. That says so much. It says that we don't pray for ourselves unless we are praying that God use us for the growth of someone else. But right now we want to ask that we have the knowledge of His will. This is where we pray that we might listen quietly for the still small voice that already dwells in each of our hearts (the Kingdom of God lies within) and comes to light the more we make time for it to speak. The more you get attuned to listening, the more you will hear and be led. There is no doubt about it. It takes time and practice. For the depressed person like yourself you will find that the only voices you heard were the old tapes that kept playing in your head, reminding you how bad and worthless you were. Now you are hearing how, if you trust in the Higher Power, you will begin to feel better.

Talk to God about how you can get out of the pit that you're in – then listen. In time you can hear the solution to your question. This is a trust relationship with your God.

A recovering alcoholic said:

In the twelve steps the word God is mentioned seven times, but the particular addiction – alcohol, drugs, gambling, etc. – is only mentioned once, in the first step. After a while you become so close to God, you really depend on Him not just at prayer time but all day long. (1)

We want only to know God's will because if your will is lined up with God's will, then everything that you need or want is all there. It's very liberating to desire only that your will be in God's will. The more you pray, the more you will want to be in God's will. Your *sadd*iction will be a thing of the past and the peace of God will be a thing of the *now*.

We are able to heal the sadness that goes deep into our very soul only by the surrender of ourselves to the Higher Power and by trusting our sadness and despair to the members of the twelve-step group. You begin to feel completely and unconditionally accepted by this group of people involved with their issues – many times going all the way back to a childhood in which they were unloved and abandoned. Some were not physically abandoned, like a parent leaving home or a parent dying – they were abandoned in the sense that no one ever loved them and told them how special they were. We know that it is this feeling of being abandoned that sets us up for our addictions as we continue to search out someone or something to make us feel good. This great void in our lives will always leave us saddened until the day that we can name it, admit we need help and turn our life and our will over to the care of God as we understand Him. This will help us face the shame and heal the not-OKness of ourselves. We will grieve the childhood that never was and begin the work of re-parenting the child within.

Getting free from our *sadd*iction is to learn how to prize ourselves. God as we understand Him will give us the power to carry out His will for our lives. This God as you understand Him will help you put your life back together and begin to feel other emotions and energy besides the unpleasant ones so familiar to you most of your life. You can try to heal yourself on your own, but that can be very difficult. To be healed and to find acceptance for yourself is accomplished only through the power of the group. It is in the group working the twelve steps that you will find your way out of your depression. Try it and live.

We admit that our life is unmanageable and it is only when we are willing to let the Higher Power take control of our lives that we will grow and find the serenity and peace that all hearts desire. Our dependence on the Higher Power helps us become more independent of our need to sad ourselves.

Linda's Story

Hi, my name is Linda, and I am more than glad to share what DA has done for me.

I am the adult child of an alcoholic father and I seem to fit very well into the characteristics of the child of an alcoholic parent; guilt, shame, worthlessness, low self-esteem. I abhor alcohol to this day, but my addiction has become food. I am a compulsive overeater, having gained more than one hundred and fifty pounds in ten years, and I am petrified by this. I had got to the point of withdrawal from everyone, terribly lonely and very depressed. Then one weekend, when I had gone on a "binge" and was actually "drunk" on food, I hit bottom. By this I mean that I was feeling so worthless, hopeless and depressed that the thought of suicide was the only relief I could find. What really scared me was I almost found pleasure in these thoughts. After all, there would be no more pain! But deep down inside I really wanted to live – I love life and I want to live life to the fullest, but how? The depression just keeps coming and pushing at me, and a million negative thoughts that seem to completely overwhelm me at times.

Then a friend told me about DA and I was so desperate that I went and, to my surprise, these wonderful people accepted me, all of me, for myself. They encouraged me right from the start. They were open and honest about their pain and constantly reassured me that I can make it! But I would have to work very hard, because you have to really fight depression – negative thoughts replaced by positive thoughts. Action to create motivation. Most of all I had to surrender to God, quit controlling everything and everyone, including God. Let go and let God! So I started reading the Twelve Steps. At first I was really rebellious, so much so that I didn't go back for two weeks (I was too depressed, ha, ha!), but inside I knew the Steps had the key to get me out of this prison. They pointed me to my Higher Power, which unashamedly is Jesus Christ. Now I attend every meeting sharing the things I learned and the times I fall (which are still quite a few) into depression. But it is working, and I could not be writing this right now if it was not for the love and support of these very special people. As a matter of fact, I told them that once a week was not enough for me and the leader suggested that I start another one, which is just what I have done. I now attend the meetings twice a week – twice is nice!

To sum it up, DA has pointed to the only "hope" there is – our Higher Power is the only way out, He is the key, the life, the hope. And once I have been able to admit that, everyone in the group has been very loving and supportive. After all, they have all been where I am today.

Step Twelve

Having had a Spiritual Awakening as the Result of these Steps, we tried to carry this Message to Others, and to practise these Principles in all of our Affairs

The only requirement for membership in *Depressed Anonymous* is a sincere desire to quit sadding ourselves today – just for this twenty-four hour period. We want to try for this short period of time to let go of our sadness. But since we are *saddicts* we need to know that we can't just *snap out* of our sadness in minutes or even days. To get to feeling better takes time because our learning to sad ourselves goes back over months, possibly years, and one doesn't just snap out of feeling bad in a few days when this whole way of living has taken years to develop. As was brought out in another Step, it's not so much our addiction that we need to focus on as our whole *life*, which we now admit is unmanageable. By practising the principles of the twelve steps we now know that we need to make an inventory of our whole life. We can leave no rock unturned if we want to live with serenity and hope. Our sadness, like any other addiction, is merely a symptom of some deeper compulsion that manifests itself in our need to seek comfort and safety in sadness. But this is the nature of our addictive behaviour and thinking. Our thinking has been compulsive. Every time someone hurt our feelings, said something that wasn't pleasant, we withdrew into the dark hole of our depression. We shut down our feelings by numbing ourselves against future hurts. *Depressed Anonymous* wants you and me to try for one day at a time not to withdraw compulsively into sadness when we come up against a stressful situation.

We now know that it is only when we actively involve ourselves in the first step of DA that we start the march toward recovery and to living a life that can be serene and filled with hope. **Hope** is what we seek as people depressed. We refuse to label ourselves as *depressives* because we do not intend to be depressed any longer than we have to. We are also a lot more than our feelings of sadness. Our real identity is emerging from the sadness as we try to live one day at a time.

Even though we have been accustomed to live in the past and see our world as a threat and danger, we find ourselves in a fellowship of men and women who by their own admission recognize that they caused their depression and were afraid to get out of it because to experience any feeling other than sadness would be too unfamiliar and frightening.

The fellowship of DA is made up of members who

are working the programme, who have had a spiritual awakening and want to share their story of how it is now – now that they have admitted that they are *sadd*icts and how they came to believe that a power greater than themselves could restore them to sanity. This sharing from older members only gives a sense of courage to the newcomer.

We know we only have today to live our life and we want to live with *hope* today because today is all we have – yesterday is gone forever and tomorrow isn't here yet.

These twelve steps work for those who work the programme and who try to live one day at a time. Many times we have been so scared of being rejected once more that we have withdrawn deeper into the anguish of our shame and hurt. We need to air our hurts, our shame, and let others hear our story. There is something healing about hearing ourselves speak to others about our own journey in life and the many emotional potholes that we have fallen into from time to time. We have felt our lives were jinxed! But now we can begin to feel *hopeful* when other members of the group shake their heads in knowing approval of what we are saying when we tell our story. Most have been where we are now. And the more we make an effort to come to meetings regularly, the more we will find members of the group telling us how they are seeing a change in the way we act, talk and look. We will accept the group's comments as being true and honestly expressed. These people speak our language and they all have been where we are now. You gradually begin to see yourself as healer instead of victim the more you work this programme and get excited about the possibility of helping others. When you start reaching out to others in the group it is at that point that you are carrying the message of hope to others. *You have a future with Depressed Anonymous.*

We all know that any addiction and compulsive type of behaviour gradually removes you from the regular activities of persons around you, including family, friends and co-workers, until you are established in the narrow confines of pain and isolation. We are always going to be just a little more isolated the more we try to think our addiction through in the circle of our own thoughts. Most of us need the fellowship of the group to keep ourselves honest and in recovery and our dark thoughts out in the open.

Having had a spiritual awakening means that we are now aware that the core of our being is spiritual and is where our power resides. "The Kingdom of God is within you." This spiritual awakening occurred when we finally let the God of our understanding enter our lives and we surrendered our resistance to getting better. We soon discover in the programme that no compulsion can be controlled by will power alone – it must be surrendered to the Higher Power or to the care of God as we understand Him. It alone will remove in time the burden from our backs. This is the spiritual awakening that keeps us free from sadness as we take the message of healing to others in the group who are new to the programme. We admit that we make no promises to anyone and that there will be no magic answers and quick solutions to their *sadd*iction. No, it all takes time and this is the message of the group – such slogans as – *Take it easy – Keep it simple – Easy does it* – are all meant to help you and me to live one day at a time and continue to try to live with serenity. When we practise these steps on a daily basis, starting our day with asking the Higher Power for guidance for the rest of the day, we can then be assured of His presence and help in our lives.

When you have walked the programme and worked the Steps and turned your life over to God as you understand Him you will springclean and make amends where needed and let the Higher Power be manifest in your life.

We don't need to call or label someone a *sadd*ict – let them discover that themselves after they hear our own stories. We want to tell them the way it was before DA and how it is now that we are living the DA twelve-step programme. Once newcomers hear the before and after of our lives it will make it easier for them to believe us when they experience our own enthusiasm and cheerfulness. They will believe that our recovery isn't put on. Also our hopeful witness to our recovery is the best witness that the twelve-step programme works. There are two kinds of *sadd*icts: 1) the recovering *sadd*ict, viz., the one who is working the twelve-step programme and is aware of how his/her addiction to sadness is ruining his/her life; and 2) the miserable *sadd*ict, viz., the one who continues to deny and/or rationalizes that he/she can choose to feel something different from sadness.

Both you and the new man [and woman] must walk day by day in the path of spiritual progress. If you persist, remarkable things will happen. When we look back, we realize that the things which came to us when we put ourselves in God's hands were better than anything we could have planned. Follow the dictates of a Higher Power and you will presently live in a new and wonderful world, no matter what your present circumstances. (1)

What a promise!

Remarkable things happen to us when we are willing

to admit defeat and talk about our powerlessness over our depression and how our lives had become unmanageable. This first step is the beginning of the flight of steps that takes us up and into our new way of living. At our fellowship of DA we talk **hope**, we act **hopeful**, we think **hope**. We learn that our thinking depressed and negative thoughts might have got us in the shape that we are in today. What you think is what you become. For us who find sadness our second nature we at times continue to revert to the comfort of old familiar negative thinking and are in actuality returning to self-destructive activity. Sadness is overcome by **hope**.

When we became convinced that a power greater than ourselves could restore us to sanity we found ourselves turning many times during a twenty-four-hour period to that power. It is a rock in a rocky sea that we all hold on to when we find it easier just to give up and sad ourselves, instead of facing the storm and living through the fear. What Bill W. said about the alcoholic applies equally to the *sadd*ict.

He (she) can settle for mediocrity and self-satisfaction even though this may indeed prove to be a precarious perch. Or he (she) can choose to go on growing in greatness of spirit and action.

You never stop using and following the steps of the programme – we are in recovery all our lives. You don't graduate. When we return to sadding ourselves we return to the old compulsion that can again reduce us to that bankrupt individual who is bereft of peace and **hope**. We want to grow in the conviction that the Higher Power will restore us to sanity. One of the best ways to grow out of our *sadd*iction is to start acting the healer instead of being the passive victim. We are under the care of no one except our God as we understand Him.

This spiritual awakening is enhanced even further when we make a decision to turn our wills and our minds over to the care of God as we understand Him. Without a doubt this is a very big step for many people, viz., to trust anybody – and now especially a God whom they have spent a lifetime fearing. It is this decision which allows us to feel freedom when we start to practise the daily turning over of our will to God. It frees us up, and as we pray and listen in our meditation times we find that our spiritual capacity to connect with the Higher Power is greatly magnified.

Now we have to look at ourselves and do some springcleaning. We have to start listening to others in the group when they talk about Steps Four and Five, because these are the critical steps that free us from the guilt, shame and burdens of perfectionism and the need to control that we have carried within ourselves all these years. The practice of making this fearless and moral inventory of ourselves on a daily basis, especially at the end of our day, brings us up to date on how we have been living the programme. It also helps us take an active role in removing the bricks that make up the walls of our prison of depression.

Practising these principles keeps us in tune on a daily basis with the God as we understand Him, and helps us keep our **hope** strong enough so that we can move away from our compulsion to sad ourselves. When we are within the fellowship of DA we learn how we are the ones responsible for our recovery, and that we can't blame our spouses, children, co-workers or anyone else for our depressed state.

Humility is the response to honesty. The more honest we

are, the more we are willing and able to think humbly about ourselves. Over time our narcissistic attitudes will gradually wither away as we continue to deal honestly with our lives and work the twelve-step programme.

Making a list of everyone we had hurt and being willing to make amends to them all is another road to serenity and happiness. We are willing to clear out all the wreckage of our past lives, with our resentments and hurts being admitted up front. We also need to ask forgiveness from all those whom we felt rejected us.

Making direct amends and taking a personal inventory continues our progress in the programme and helps free us from all the hurts of the past. We know now that we can't afford to think long about real or imagined hurts, or we will throw ourselves back into sadding ourselves once again. And any time we want to stop and reflect on how badly other people have treated us, we need to reflect on what we are doing to ourselves by all this negative rehashing. We are giving in to a compulsion that leads us down a path that is darkness, isolation and pain. The more we take an inventory of our actions, thoughts and feelings, the more we will be forewarned about those thoughts that we previously had saddened our lives with.

Just the feeling that we want to withdraw from everyone is a warning signal that we need to get to a meeting, talk to a friend and get moving. It is our efforts to face the risk of living with the unpredictable that will free us from sadding ourselves.

Depressed Anonymous is not the place to have people feel sorry for you; *Depressed Anonymous* is a spiritual programme where you will find people like yourself, honestly, openly and willingly dealing with their character defects and gradually admitting that they will have to change their lives and lifestyle if they are going to be a whole and honest human being. The decision is yours. You make the choice! The twelve steps and your own personal story can now be shared with others and can help them on their own life's journey.

The promises of Alcoholics Anonymous apply equally well to those who are working the same twelve steps in *Depressed Anonymous*.

> If we are painstaking about this phase of our development, we will be amazed before we are halfway through. We are going to know a new happiness. We will not regret the past nor wish to shut the door on it. We will comprehend the word "serenity" and we will know peace. No matter how far down the scale we have gone, we will see how our experience can benefit others. That feeling of uselessness and self-pity will disappear. We will lose interest in selfish things and gain interest in our fellows. Self-seeking will slip away. Our whole attitude and outlook upon life will change. Fear of people and of economic insecurity will leave us. We will intuitively know how to handle situations which used to baffle us. We will suddenly realize that God is doing for us what we could not do for ourselves. . . .
>
> Are these extravagant promises? We think not. They are being fulfilled among us – sometimes quickly, sometimes slowly. They will always materialize if we work for them. (1)

These promises indeed are true and we know they are true because of the witness of the thousands upon thousands of addicted people who are now free from their compulsions because of working the twelve steps every day of their lives. Those people who have worked the twelve steps – for any addiction imaginable – have found that their compulsion has been defeated and they are recovering their very best selves.

I thank God every day for my freedom from my addiction, and I am now able to share my story of how God as I understand Him is working in my life with other members of the DA group. My healing, like yours, is now being passed along to all those persons whose depression has made their lives unmanageable. With our new found belief in a power greater than ourselves we are living manifestations of God's power at work.

Thy will be done!

Step Thirteen

How to start a

Depressed Anonymous Group

If there is a DA group operating near where you live you could go to one of their meetings, but if yours will be the first in your area you might find it helpful to attend one or two other self-help groups just to see how they operate. Most self-help groups, as well as DA, have literature about their work which you would find helpful.

Once you have three or four people who, like you, are struggling with depression and who want to set up a DA group which will follow the twelve-step programme, you can form a core group to work out how to contact other people, where you will meet and when, and how you will all share the work and the responsibility of the group.

Sometimes a professional person – a doctor, psychologist, social worker, psychiatric nurse, or a minister of religion – is keen to get such a group started, or would be most sympathetic if you asked for help to get one going. You must make it clear from the start that this is a self-help group. If the professional person wants to attend the group it should be as an equal member of it and not as its leader, or as an observer. However, in establishing the group the professional may be able to help in providing a place for it to meet and advising about organizing the group's finances.

Again, when you contact your local Health Centres and Community Mental Health Teams to let them know you are setting up the group, make it clear that this is a self-help group and, while you would like their support, you do not want them to take it over.

To contact other likely members, draw up a notice which states the aims of the group, who the group is for, the time, day and place of meeting, and the name and phone number of the group member (or members) who can give more information about the group and who will arrange to meet and welcome new members. When you are depressed it is often very difficult to go into a room full of strangers, so having someone meet you beforehand can be a great help.

Send copies of this notice to

* Health Centres
* Community Mental Health Teams
* Local General Practitioners
* Social Services
* Health Visitors
* Probation Department
* Pastoral Care departments of churches
* Local ministers of religion
* Local radio stations
* Local newspapers, including free ones
* Local library
* Local post offices and shops which carry notices
* Local Mental Health Association

* Local branch of Samaritans
* Other self-help groups

Many people believe they are the only ones going through this painful experience that we call depression. When they discover that there is a group of people who feel as they do this in itself can provide hope. In time and with regular attendance at *Depressed Anonymous* meetings they will no longer feel like victims but will reach out and be healers.

If surrender of our wills to the "care of God" is of the essence of the spiritual life, for anyone who truly desires to free himself/herself from a chronic and compulsive behaviour such as depression then the twelve steps can be your stepping stones to the path of a hope-filled life.

Chairperson's guide for leading
Depressed Anonymous meeting

Leader

(Each group member takes it in turn to be leader.)

"Good evening, my name is (*first name only*) and I want to welcome you all to *Depressed Anonymous*, a twelve-step programme of recovery. We are a self-help group where people with similar needs can generate new positive energies . . .   form   networks   of   friendship   and support . . . give each other the strength to live each new day with hope. We are a self-help group and as such we are not professionally led and we aim to be self-supporting."

Leader explains how his/her life was before DA and how

it is now since he/she has been coming to meetings and working the twelve steps.

1   Serenity Prayer is said by all: **God, grant me the serenity to accept the things I cannot change . . . The courage to change the things I can . . . And the wisdom to know the difference**.

2   **Leader** reads the Statements of Concern.

3   Twelve steps passed around the group. Each person reads a step. Then the twelve traditions are passed around the group. Each person reads a tradition.

4   The **Leader** invites a volunteer to read *How DA Works*.

5   **Leader**: "I want to welcome all new persons tonight. We all hope that you find the experience here a most helpful one."

6   **Leader**: "I invite each member in turn to share his/her last week's experiences with depression, and each person's sharing should be no longer than five minutes in length. People can say 'Pass' if they don't feel like sharing."

7   The **Leader** then opens the meeting to the whole group. (If the meeting is the first one of the month then one of the twelve steps is discussed. This is what is called the *step meeting*.) The **Leader** chooses the topic for this meeting, either from one of the twelve steps, the twelve traditions or a topic appropriate for the meeting.

8   After an hour or so of meeting the **Leader** gives each member a chance to say *what she/he hopes to do positively for themselves by the next meeting*. Each person states his/her activity goal for the coming week. Each member of the group also comments briefly on *one hopeful/positive statement that struck him/her in particular at this meeting*.

9 Meeting offering box is passed around to support needs and expenses of the group.

10 Leader makes announcements and one person volunteers to be Leader for next week's meeting.

11 Leader has members rise and hold hands as they close the meeting with The Lord's Prayer, or any other prayer, poem, or statement which the group feels affirms their belief.

Depressed Anonymous statements of concern

1 DA is not a replacement for an individual's relationship with his/her therapist.

2 DA believes that, if you are taking some medication, you should continue to do so until you and your doctor agree that this medication is no longer necessary. You must exercise *your right to know* from your doctor about all potential side-effects of this medication and any literature from the manufacturer that would be helpful to you the consumer. *It's your health!*

3 Since many experiences of depression are due to a real or perceived loss, divorce, death of spouse, loss of a job, health, cherished possession, or loss of a love, it helps to believe that as an active member of DA you can live through this period of depression and become the happy person you want to be.

4 Anonymity is not just a question of our name. It's

an essential element in recovery. It is helpful for the depressed to feel that they can come forward without revealing their identity. Perhaps even more importantly, anonymity stresses the unity of DA – which depends on the acceptance that we are all equal in the fellowship. Anonymity reminds us to place principle above personality.

> WHOM YOU SEE HERE,
> WHAT YOU HEAR HERE,
> WHEN YOU LEAVE HERE,
> LET IT STAY HERE.

The Twelve Steps of **Depressed Anonymous**

1   We admitted that we were powerless over depression – that our lives had become unmanageable.

2   Came to believe that a Power greater than ourselves could restore us to sanity.

3   Made a decision to turn our will and our lives over to the care of God, *as we understood Him*.

4   Made a searching and fearless moral inventory of ourselves.

5   Admitted to God, to ourselves and to another human being the exact nature of our wrongs.

6   Were entirely ready to have God remove all these defects of character.

7   Humbly asked Him to remove our shortcomings.

8   Made a list of all persons we had harmed, and became willing to make amends to them all.

9   Made direct amends to such people wherever possible, except when to do so would injure them or others.

10   Continued to take a personal inventory and when we were wrong promptly admitted it.

11   Sought through prayer and meditation to improve our conscious contact with God as we understood Him, praying only for knowledge of His will for us and the power to carry it out.

12   Having had a spiritual awakening as the result of these steps, we tried to carry the message to other depressed persons and to practise these principles in all of our affairs.

The Twelve Traditions of Depressed Anonymous

1   Our common welfare should come first; personal progress depends upon DA unity.

2   For our group purposes there is but one ultimate authority – a loving God as He may express Himself in our group conscience. Our leaders are but trusted servants; they do not govern.

3   The only requirement for DA membership is a desire to stop sadding ourselves.

4   Each group should be autonomous except in matters affecting other groups or DA as a whole.

5   Each group has but one primary purpose – to carry its message to the depressed person who is still miserable.

6 A DA group should never endorse, finance or lend the DA name to any related facility or outside enterprise, lest problems of money, property and prestige divert us from our primary purpose.

7 Every DA group ought to be fully self-supporting, declining outside contributions.

8 *Depressed Anonymous* should remain forever non-professional, but our service centres may employ special workers.

9 DA as such ought never be organized; but we may create service boards or committees directly responsible to those they serve.

10 *Depressed Anonymous* has no opinion on outside issues; hence the DA name ought never to be drawn into public controversy.

11 Our public relations policy is based on attraction rather than promotion; we need always to maintain personal anonymity at the level of press, radio and films.

12 Anonymity is the spiritual foundation of our traditions, ever reminding us to place principles before personalities.

How **DA** works

You are about to witness the miracle of the group. You are joining a group of people who are on a journey of hope and who mutually care for each other. You will hear how hope, light and energy have been regained by those who were hopeless and in a black hole and tired of living.

By our involvement in the group we are feeling that

there is hope – there is a chance for me too – I can get better. But we are not the people with the magic pills and the easy formulas for success. We believe that to get out of the prison of depression takes time and work.

We have all been wounded in different degrees by the experience of depression. We also know that there is a method to regain control over our lives that is practical and workable. It is successful for all those who want to change their lives. We once believed that there was no hope and that suicide was the only way out.

In this natural world one of the first laws is that all growth is gradual – that belief is the bottom line for all of us who are depressed, and who want to get better. The more we attend meetings the more we will learn and see the various ways to escape from depression. We also learn how important it is to not give up on ourselves.

How do I know if I'm depressed?

Being depressed means *isolation*, being cut off from everybody and everything. People describe their experience of depression as being in some kind of a prison. One man said that he was in a pit where the walls were of soft clay – the more he tried to climb up the more he slid back down. One woman said that she was in a brick maze where there was no exit and the walls were closing in on her. "I'm in an infinite desert," said one man, "there's just me and a lone, scrawny tree." "I'm in a cage," said one woman, "the bars are thick and black and there's no door." Inside this prison the person has intense feelings of self-hatred.

Inside the prison of depression the person can experience the following –

* Changes in appetite.
* Shifts in sleeping patterns (too much/not enough sleep).
* Waking up early in the morning.
* Fatigability or lack of energy.
* Agitation or increased activity.
* Loss of interest in daily activities and/or decreased sex drive.
* Feeling of sadness, hopelessness, worthlessness, guilt or self-reproach and possible thoughts about killing oneself.
* Withdrawing from others and wanting to be alone most of the time.
* Weeping/not being able to cry.
* Lapses of memory.
* Hard time making decisions.
* Fear of losing one's mind.
* Reluctance to take any risks.

For more information concerning *Depressives Anonymous* please write, sending a stamped, self-addressed envelope to,

Depressives Anonymous
36 Chestnut Avenue,
Beverley,
North Humberside,
HU17 9QU

Depressives Associated
PO Box 5,
Castle Town,
Portland,
Dorset, DT5 1BQ

For information about *Depressed Anonymous* please write (with a stamped, self-addressed envelope, to:

Depressed Anonymous
Co-ordinator: Hugh Smith
1013 Wagner Avenue,
Louisville, KY 40217, USA
(502) 637–8210

The AntiDepressant Tablet (A Quarterly Publication)
Editor: Hugh Smith
1013 Wagner Avenue,
Louisville, KY 40217, USA
(502) 637–8210

Frances's Story

I joined DA in 1988. At that time, I was totally depressed, with no interest in anything or anyone, and especially no interest in myself. I felt I had no worth, a feeling I had had for many years, I am sure since a child, very young.

Having lived with this feeling for so many years, I guess I thought this was normal, probably most people felt the same way. I had all the symptoms of depression but knew nothing about the sickness except to live it, which I have found to be a terrible fate, until I discovered DA.

I attend the DA meeting quite regularly. I have found that if I can attend the meetings regularly, I get the support of the members, who I have found to have about the same kind of problems as I have, maybe not quite as bad as mine, but I guess each of us feels that our problems are worse than anyone else's, I know mine are. But with the regular meetings and my friends' support, I find that I am able to manage pretty well from week to week. I have more faith in myself since I work the Twelve Steps the best that I can and trust my Higher Power (God Almighty) with all my heart. I pray to the fullest extent that I will continue to have faith in myself and others. I have become a more whole being than I have ever been. I work a lot, I volunteer a lot and have a far better outlook on life than I have ever had, and I attribute all of these good feelings to DA.

I just hope that I will always be able to attend DA meetings regularly and wish more people had the opportunity to do the same. DA has helped me so much. I cannot begin to explain sufficiently the support the meetings can give one who is depressed.

DA has been and is my salvation, and I know the Twelve-Step Programme is the only way to go to get one on the right track and it takes the meetings to keep you there. They are a "Godsend" for me and I know for a lot of others who are depressed also.

I thank DA and my Higher Power for a life worth living.

Thanks a million, Hugh, for starting *Depressed Anonymous!*

Appendix

Alcoholics Anonymous

The Twelve Steps of **Alcoholics Anonymous**

1   We admitted we were powerless over alcohol – that our *lives had become unmanageable*.

2   Came to believe that a Power greater than ourselves could restore us to sanity.

3   Made a decision to turn our will and our lives over to the care of God *as we understood Him*.

4   Made a searching and fearless moral inventory of ourselves.

5   Admitted to God, to ourselves, and to another human being the exact nature of our wrongs.

6   Were entirely ready to have God remove all these defects of character.

7   Humbly asked Him to remove our shortcomings.

8   Made a list of all persons we had harmed, and became willing to make amends to them all.

9   Made direct amends to such people wherever

possible, except when to do so would injure them or others.

10 Continued to take personal inventory and when we were wrong promptly admitted it.

11 Sought through prayer and meditation to improve our conscious contact with God *as we understood Him*, praying only for knowledge of His will for us and the power to carry that out.

12 Having had a spiritual awakening as the result of these steps, we tried to carry this message to alcoholics, and to practise these principles in all our affairs.

(The Twelve Steps reprinted and adapted with permission of Alcoholics Anonymous World Services, Inc.)

The Twelve Traditions of **Alcoholics Anonymous**

1 Our common welfare should come first; personal recovery depends upon AA unity.

2 For our purpose there is but one ultimate authority – a loving God as He may express Himself in our group conscience. Our leaders are but trusted servants; they do not govern.

3 The only requirement for AA membership is a desire to stop drinking.

4 Each group should be autonomous except in matters affecting other groups or AA as a whole.

5 Each group has but one primary purpose – to carry its message to the alcoholic who still suffers.

6 An AA group ought never to endorse, finance, or lend the AA name to any related facility or outside enterprise, lest problems of money, property, and prestige divert us from our primary purpose.

7 Every AA group ought to be fully self-supporting, declining outside contributions.

8 Alcoholics Anonymous should remain forever nonprofessional, but our service centres may employ special workers.

9 AA as such ought never be organized; but we may create service boards or committees directly responsible to those they serve.

10 Alcoholics Anonymous has no opinion on outside issues; hence the AA name ought never be drawn into public controversy.

11 Our public relations policy is based on attraction rather than promotion; we need always maintain personal anonymity at the level of press, radio and films.

12 Anonymity is the spiritual foundation of all our traditions, ever reminding us to place principles before personalities.

(The twelve traditions reprinted and adapted with permission of Alcoholics Anonymous World Services, Inc.)

Glossary

counsellor   A person who has taken courses in counselling, the skill of listening to, empathizing with, and supporting people in need of such help.

denial   A defence mechanism that simply disavows or denies thoughts, feelings, wishes or needs that cause the person holding them anxiety.

projection   A defence mechanism where one's own feelings, needs, wishes, emotions, beliefs are seen as being possessed by another person.

psychiatrist   A person trained in medicine who specializes in the prevention, diagnosis and treatment of mental disorders. The actual practice of the psychiatrist and the clinical psychologist overlap considerably; the primary difference being that the psychiatrist, by virtue of the medical licence, is legally authorized to prescribe drugs while the clinical psychologist is not.

psychoanalyst   A person who has had psychoanalytic training at a recognized institute. Psychoanalysts may have had any of a number of different forms of training prior to the psychoanalytical, e.g., a medical degree with post-graduate psychiatric training, a post-graduate degree in psychology or social work. The term *lay analyst* is often used for practitioners who have not taken a medical degree.

psychologist A person who holds a degree in psychology which is recognized by the British Psychological Society. Psychologists registered with the British Psychological Society are called Chartered Psychologists. A *clinical psychologist* is a qualified psychologist who has specialized in the diagnosis and therapy of people who have some problems in coping with their lives.

psychology is the study of why people and animals behave as they do.

psychotherapist A person who practises psychotherapy, that is, any technique or procedure that has palliative or curative effects upon any mental, emotional or behavioural disorder.

rationalization A defence mechanism whereby things which are confusing or unacceptable are made to appear clear, concise and rational.

Bibliography

1 *Alcoholics Anonymous: The Story of How Men and Women Have Recovered from Alcoholism*, Alcoholics Anonymous World Services, Inc., New York, 1955.

2 A Co-founder of AA, *Alcoholics Anonymous Comes of Age: A Brief History of Alcoholics Anonymous*, Alcoholics Anonymous World Services, Inc., New York, 1957.

3 A Co-Founder of AA, *Twelve Steps and Twelve Traditions*, Alcoholics Anonymous Services, Inc., New York, 1953.

4 A Co-Founder of AA, *As Bill Sees It: The A.A. Way of Life: Selected Writings of A.A.'s Co-Founder*, Alcoholics Anonymous World Services, Inc., New York, 1967.

5 Joan Gibson, *Open the Window: Practical Ideas for the Lonely and Depressed*, Gateway Books, Bath (UK) and Interbook, San Leandro (USA), 1985.

6 Joan Gibson, *Living in Perspective: Facing the Enigmas of Life*, Gateway Books, Bath, 1989.

7 Alister Hardy, *The Spiritual Nature of Man*, Clarendon Press, Oxford, 1979.

8 David Hay, *Exploring Inner Space: Scientists and Religious Experience*, Penguin, London, 1981.

9 Aldous Huxley, *The Perennial Philosophy*, Chatto and Windus, London, 1946.

10 Lao Tzu, *The Tao te Ching*, translated by Stephen Mitchell, Macmillan, London, 1989.

11 Alice Miller, *The Drama of Being a Child*, Virago, London, 1989.

12 Alice Miller, *For Your Own Good: Hidden Cruelty in Child-rearing and the Roots of Violence*, Virago, London, 1989.

13 Alice Miller, *Thou Shalt Not Be Aware: Society's Betrayal of the Child*, Virago, London, 1989.

14 Alice Miller, *The Untouched Key: Tracing Childhood Trauma in Creativity and Destructiveness*, Virago, London, 1990.

15 Alice Miller, *Banished Knowledge: Facing Childhood Injuries*, Virago, London, 1990.

16 Stanton Peele (ed.), *Visions of Addiction: Major Contemporary Perspectives on Addiction and Alcoholism*, Lexington Books, Heath and Company, Lexington, MASS (USA), 1988.

17 Dorothy Rowe, *Depression: the Way Out of Your Prison*, Routledge, London, 1983.

18 Dorothy Rowe, *Living with the Bomb: Can We Live without Enemies?*, Routledge, London, 1985.

19 Dorothy Rowe, *Beyond Fear*, Fontana, London, 1987.

20 Dorothy Rowe, *Choosing Not Losing*, Fontana, London, 1988.

21 Dorothy Rowe, *The Successful Self*, Fontana, London, 1988.

22 Dorothy Rowe, *The Construction of Life and Death*, Fontana, London, 1989.

23 Dorothy Rowe, *The Depression Handbook*, Fontana, London, 1991.

24 Dorothy Rowe, *Wanting Everything*, Fontana, London, 1991.

25 Hugh Smith, *Foxbarr*, Wilmot Enterprise, Wilmot, SD (USA), 1980.

26 Hugh Smith, *Your Special Giftedness: A Spiritual Gifts Inventory*, Wilmot Enterprise, Wilmot, SD (USA), 1985.

27 *Webster's New World Dictionary*, Third College Edition.